PENNSYLVANIA'S COLDEST CASES

Pennsylvania's Coldest Cases

Ten Unsolved Murders That Rocked the Keystone State

Marlin Bressi

Essex, Connecticut

Globe
Pequot

An imprint of The Globe Pequot Publishing Group, Inc.
64 South Main Street
Essex, CT 06426
www.GlobePequot.com

Distributed by NATIONAL BOOK NETWORK

British Library Cataloguing in Publication Information available

Library of Congress Cataloging-in-Publication Data available
ISBN 978-1-4930-8825-6 (paper: alk. paper)
ISBN 978-1-4930-8826-3 (electronic)

♾™ The paper used in this publication meets the minimum requirements of American National Standard for Information Sciences—Permanence of Paper for Printed Library Materials, ANSI/ NISO Z39.48-1992.

CONTENTS

Introduction

Widely considered the first modern detective story, Edgar Allan Poe's "The Murders in the Rue Morgue" was published in 1841. Since then, murder mysteries have continued to captivate American audiences, from the silent era to the streaming era, from the bright lights of Broadway to the stage of your local dinner theater. A walk through the aisles of your favorite bookstore offers an all-you-can-read buffet of murder and mystery in all its tantalizing flavors. With the genre of "true crime" flourishing thanks to countless podcasts and cable documentaries, it would take a dozen lifetimes to devour it all. So much crime, so little time!

While we tend to view the true crime genre as a modern creation, literary accounts of real-life robberies and murders can be found in English broadsides and pamphlets dating back to the sixteenth century, emphasizing the timeless nature of the genre. When it comes to mysteries, those left unsolved linger in the minds of readers long after the final sentence has been read. The lack of a neat and satisfying conclusion, as seen with unsolved murders in detective novels, leaves the audience with a world of possibilities.

Pennsylvania's Coldest Cases focuses particularly on murder cases, which captivate the public with their unique angles and peculiar details. The title itself is a double entendre, as it refers both to the elapsed time since these chilling crimes were committed, as well as the horrendous manner in which the unfortunate victims met their demise. From the ten murders highlighted, there's the case of Doris Whittmore, a friendly and well-liked prostitute whose lifeless body was carried into her apartment in the dead of night and arranged neatly in her bed. Not only is the identity of her killer unknown, but the location and exact manner of her death are also shrouded in mystery. There's the case of the Hershey Torch Murder, in which a body was placed into a car and the vehicle set on fire to look like an accident. While the owner of the vehicle was eventually convicted of insurance fraud, he refused to say who the body belonged to or how he had acquired it. There's the case of Henry and Ruth Shearer, a happily married New York couple found along a Lycoming County stream with their throats cut, 150 miles from home, while their young daughter remained inside their parked automobile just a few feet away. And then there's the case of Norman Bechtel, a Mennonite church worker whose body was found near an abandoned mansion with occult symbols carved into his face.

These are among the ten baffling murders chosen for their bizarre details and unusual circumstances found in this book, and while I have furnished most of the story for you, it is up to your imagination to figure out the ending. If you can "crack the case," you will have succeeded where hundreds of our best and brightest detectives have failed.

The Feely Triple Death Mystery

ALLEGHENY COUNTY

A charming variety of early twentieth-century architectural styles delights the eyes of motorists driving along South Braddock Avenue in the Point Breeze neighborhood of Pittsburgh. Behind banks of billowing greenery are Prairie-style brick homes and enchanting American Craftsman bungalows with overhanging eaves, interrupted by the occasional Mediterranean-style dwelling with dazzling white stucco walls. However, there is one house perched atop a hill that appears as an anomaly, with its distinctive Queen Anne turret and gabled roof; what makes this dwelling unique, apart from its anachronistic style, is the fact that it is a murder house. To be more accurate, it is a triple murder house and the site of one of the most baffling mysteries in Pittsburgh history.

In 1936, this house at 312 South Braddock Avenue was a luxury apartment home occupied by the family of the owner, Charles Young, and a respectable family named Feely. Described as the "ideal family," the Feelys consisted of Martin, his wife Eleanor, and their two young children, Bobby and Janice. By all accounts, the family was the envy of the neighborhood; handsome and rugged Martin J. Feely was a physical education professor at the University of Pittsburgh, while his wife was a graduate of Columbia University in New York. The orphan daughter of wealthy and sophisticated parents, "Andy," as Eleanor was known to her friends, seemed to have the world on a platter. She was young, intelligent, athletic, and beautiful. She held degrees in law, child psychology, and physical education. Yet, she put her career on hold to get married and start a family. Eleanor Buckley and Martin Feely were married at Christmastime in 1931 in a charming chapel in Valley Forge, and she quickly settled into a life of utter contentment with her handsome and dynamic husband and her young children. Marty, Andy, Bobby, and Jan—the perfect all-American family. Or so everyone believed.

Five-year-old Bobby, three-year-old Janice, and Eleanor were found brutally slain inside their apartment on June 18, 1936, while Martin was away from home. But who would want to slaughter Eleanor Feely and her two young children? To this day, no one is quite sure who carried out this diabolical act, though some suspect that Eleanor might have been the culprit, while others insisted that the husband, Martin, had orchestrated the tragedy.

"Why, it was the most perfect marriage I ever knew—an entirely wholesome relationship," remarked Thelma Mertz, a family friend who worked as a secretary at the University of Pittsburgh's Physical Education School. "Marty was born to be married," added Mertz. "He was the most completely married man I know!" John Dambach, who was Martin's superior in the physical education department and one of his closest friends, expressed similar sentiments. He remembered the time when Martin came to live with him for a few weeks when Bobby was infected with scarlet fever. Eleanor didn't want her husband to catch it, so she implored him to stay with his colleague. According to Dambach, the young man seemed "utterly lost" without his family by his side.

On June 6, Martin had left Pittsburgh for the Life Magazine Boys Camp in Pottersville, New Jersey, of which he was a director. Before departing, he left a note for his secretary, Miss Mertz: Out for lunch. Back September 21. Martin's family was to join him in New Jersey on June 19. On the eve of their planned departure, Jan, Bobby, and Eleanor were found dead inside their seven-room, first-floor luxury apartment. The rooms were in perfect order, and all the windows, except for one, were latched from the inside. No fingerprints had been left behind on the doors, knobs, or windowsills. There were no signs of struggle, no reports of screams by the neighbors. Nothing of value had been removed from the premises. Naturally, suspicion immediately fell upon Eleanor Feely.

THE DEATH SCENE

It was the landlord, Charles Young, who discovered the crime scene early on the morning of Thursday, June 18. The forty-eight-year-old landlord, who lived in the third-floor apartment with his wife and their seventeen-year-old son Fred, told authorities that he couldn't sleep because he hadn't seen or heard from the Feelys for almost twenty-four hours. Knowing that Bobby had recently been stricken with scarlet fever, Young began to worry over the curious silence. He telephoned a mutual friend, a high school teacher named Austin Grupe, believing that Eleanor and her children might be there. They were not. Young put on a robe, grabbed a flashlight, and went down to the terrace that slopes around the sprawling old house to check on his tenants. The back and front wooden doors were wide open, though the screen doors in front of them were latched from the inside. He knew at that moment something was not right. Working up his courage, he shone his light through one of the bedroom windows, and what he saw chilled his blood.

The landlord found Eleanor face down in a pool of blood from a stab wound, tied to a radiator pipe with a hemp rope that had been fastened around her neck. Into this rope the handle of a claw hammer had been twisted until Eleanor was strangled. When the police arrived, they found the hammer under her body. The light of the flashlight revealed that the children were in the same room, strangled to death before an ice pick had been jammed into their skulls. Bobby lay on his back on a cot, wearing khaki overalls with his name embroidered in red thread, and the cord from a bathrobe tied tightly around his neck. Janice was in her crib, face up, dressed in blue and white flowered pajamas. A hemp rope had been wound tightly around her neck as well. The ice pick was on the floor to the right of Eleanor.

After viewing the gory spectacle through the window, Young raced up to the second floor, which was occupied by his father-in-law, and telephoned the police. When they arrived, Young snipped a hole in the door screen, lifted the latch, and let them inside. In addition to the hammer and ice pick, they discovered a red-handled screwdriver beneath Janice's body and dishes and a butcher knife on the table. Their luggage had already been packed in preparation for their trip to New Jersey.

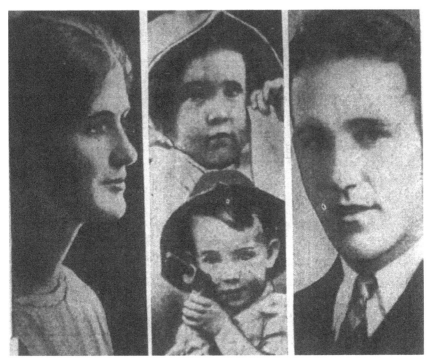

The Feely Family. From left: Eleanor, Janice (center top), Bobby (center bottom) and Martin. *Shenandoah Evening Herald*, June 23, 1936.

Pointing to the lack of fingerprints on the doors and windows and the lack of clues pointing to a forced entry, city detectives immediately concluded that it had been a case of murder-suicide. James Davidson, the county ballistics expert, and Inspector Howard Forner agreed. The deputy coroner, however, scoffed at this notion. According to Deputy Coroner John Artz, Eleanor had been tied to the radiator with a sailor's square knot—hardly the kind of knot a woman would use. In addition, all three victims had been stabbed in the left temple. If the mother had been right-handed, it would've been unnatural for her to stab herself in the left temple; if she had been left-handed, it would be equally unnatural to stab the children in the left temple. Also, detectives discovered one thumbprint on the hammer, and it did not belong to Eleanor Feely.

"I don't care what the police say," declared Deputy Coroner Artz. "Some fiend—some ghoul—murdered these three." The landlord, along with friends, relatives, and neighbors, agreed with Artz. Also adhering to this theory was Grace Stansbury, the nurse who had lived at the home during Bobby's illness.

"I can't believe she would end her own life," said Stansbury, "and certainly she would not kill those darling children." The nurse readily admitted that Mrs. Feely was high-strung and anxious at times, and even depressed, but Stansbury chalked it up to worry over Bobby's illness. "He was the loveliest child I ever nursed," she said. One thing that Artz and the police could agree on was that Eleanor, Bobby, and Janice had been dead for hours. The landlord hadn't seen a light inside the home since 1:00 a.m., hours before he went to check on the Feelys.

Martin Comes Home

On Friday afternoon, a devastated Martin Feely returned to Pittsburgh by train and was met by several friends, including John Dambach, who escorted Martin to the homicide bureau. "Eleanor would never have done this," was all he could manage to say. During his questioning by Sergeant Ralph Barton of the homicide squad, Martin held his hands tightly to his forehead as if he were in pain. "I knew her. I lived with her for twelve years," he wept. "She was not the kind of woman to do a radical thing like this. Who could have done it? Who could've gotten into my house?" Dazed, the devastated husband was unable to answer Barton's questions. His mind had gone blank. He kept asking when he could get the bodies of his wife and children.

Finding it unbearable to return to his apartment, Martin stayed with his close friend, Austin Grupe, and vowed that he would never set foot inside his home ever again. At Grupe's home a mile away on Shady Avenue, Martin sought total isolation. His meals were brought to his room by a neighbor, though he made one phone call to his wife's sister in Delaware, who had married one of his old friends from college. He did return to his South Braddock Avenue home, briefly, but refused to enter the room where the killings took place, and he refused to speak to reporters.

The Mayor Finds a Clue

Another person who wasn't satisfied with the murder-suicide theory was Pittsburgh's embattled mayor, William N. McNair, who had recently made headlines for being arrested after refusing a judge's order to refund a fine he had unlawfully assessed a citizen. The unapologetic McNair, who fashioned himself a champion of the "little guy," had a confrontational relationship with city council and the police department, which began as soon as he was sworn into office in 1934. At one point, McNair became so disillusioned with Pittsburgh politics that he set up his office in the lobby of City Hall to demonstrate his independence from the city bureaucracy. McNair also butted heads frequently with Governor George Howard Earle III, who, one year before the Feely murders, cut off funding to the city over a dispute with the pugnacious mayor.

After the detectives left the crime scene without uncovering any significant clues, McNair decided that he wasn't content to sit on the sidelines. Accompanied by his wife and sister-in-law, McNair entered the property on Friday morning to snoop around, and he discovered that a Western Union messenger had inquired for the Feelys on Wednesday night. McNair telephoned the police from the Park Place Public School across the street to announce that he was "taking charge" of the investigation. He ordered the police to investigate the nature and origin of this mysterious telegram and then resumed his sleuthing with Detective Samuel Wheeler. Wheeler, who had his own troubles with city politics, had recently been demoted from inspector to detective, and his former position was given to Howard Forner, a move which many believed was an act of political cronyism. "Wheeler can work a case from the bottom up," promised the mayor, when asked about his meddling in the Feely case. "Wheeler's a detective and Forner's a politician."

When Inspector Forner arrived at the crime scene a few hours later, McNair unceremoniously refused to let him inside. As a result, Forner and his men had no choice but to wait outside in their car while the mayor and Charles Young searched for additional clues. McNair immediately suspected that the squeaky clean condition of the apartment indicated that the crime scene had been deliberately cleaned up sometime after the murders but before the arrival of the police.

Surprisingly, the hapless and lethargic police department began to make headway in their investigation only after McNair muscled in. It was learned that the landlord had hired two "Negro handymen," William Penn of Nimmick Place and Charles Davis of Tioga Street, to renovate the apartment while the Feelys were away on vacation. Could this explain the light that was seen inside the apartment hours before Young found the bodies? With the departure of Mrs. Feely and the children planned for the next morning, it's likely both men had already been given keys to the property and, being handymen, this could also explain where the rope, screwdriver, and claw hammer came from. But there was one glaring problem with this theory—nothing had been stolen from the apartment. And, surely, the sudden appearance of two unknown men in the dead of night would elicit cries of alarm from one of the Feelys, if not all three.

McNair, however, wasn't about to rule out anything—or anyone—and Inspector Forner had to reluctantly admit to the press that he was no longer sure about his suicide theory.

A BULLDOG AND A BOTTLE OF MILK

The best chance of solving the mystery was the fingerprint found on the hammer, but experts eventually concluded that the thumbprint belonged to one of the police officers who had carelessly handled the evidence. This enraged Mayor McNair, who roared, "Nothing should have been touched in this house until this mystery was cleaned up, and it looks like a mystery to me."

The post-mortem examination, performed by Dr. R. M. Helmbold, provided some additional facts, though it did not provide any answers. The stab wounds the victims had suffered were not fatal, and an additional shallow stab wound was found on Eleanor's chest. Bobby was also found to have a fractured skull, though death was caused by strangulation. This could suggest a "soft-hearted" killer, one who at least had the decency to render the child unconscious before killing him, or it could also suggest a highly motivated killer hellbent on finishing the job.

Authorities explored every angle of the case, but no motive or explanation seemed clear. Nothing was stolen from the Feely home. There were no signs of financial or domestic troubles. All members of the family

The Feelys lived on the first floor of this house at 312 South Braddock Avenue. *Pittsburgh Sun-Telegraph*, June 19, 1936.

were healthy and of sound mind, and even little Bobby had made a full recovery from his illness. The Feelys had no known enemies, and there were no signs of a forced entry. The two handymen hired by the land-lord had alibis. Martin could offer no information that detectives didn't already know. The only possible explanation was that Eleanor, Janice, and Bobby had been murdered by someone who was known to them, and a bulldog and a bottle of milk might prove this theory.

After the tragedy had occurred, landlord Charles Young recalled that his bulldog, Toots, didn't bark during the night of the South Braddock Avenue massacre. "If there had been a struggle, we would have heard," said Young. "If not, our bulldog, Toots, certainly would. Toots didn't bark at all." According to ballistics expert (and deputy coroner) James Davidson, he saw a full bottle of milk on the kitchen counter, suggesting that Eleanor had brought it inside from the back porch for a breakfast that was never eaten. Considering the time of day, the only people who were inside the house when the murder took place were Young, his wife, his teenage son, and Alois Schaffner, Young's father-in-law.

DROPPED LIKE A HOT POTATO

On Saturday, June 20, two brothers of Eleanor Feely, Robert and Richard Buckley, arrived in Pittsburgh on a charter plane from New York to view their sister's body and urge the police to intensify their search for the killer. At the morgue, they identified the body and pointed out that Eleanor never used her left hand, which led the Buckley brothers to refute the suicide theory. The stab wound on Eleanor's left temple could not have been self-inflicted, they insisted. John Black, supervisor of the morgue, wasn't so sure. He had seen stranger things during his long career. "It's not suicide!" declared Robert to the press. "My sister was dearly devoted to her children. Dearly attached to them and happily married."

The suicide theory was also doubted by a pair of sisters from nearby McKees Rocks who had worked for the Feelys as domestic servants. Pearl and Mary Kozak had also gone to the morgue to view the bodies and had burst into tears at the terrible sight. "They were the finest people we ever knew," said Pearl. "They never had a disagreement and were always happy together." Of course, history is filled with stories about seemingly perfect couples with dark secrets and shocking double lives. Were Martin and Eleanor truly as happy as they appeared? And while there is no rule that states that a suicide victim must leave behind a note, no such note was ever written by Eleanor Feely.

By the weekend, rumors and innuendo were running rampant through the city, especially after it was reported that Martin had made arrangements for the bodies of his wife and children to be cremated and their ashes scattered in an undisclosed location after a memorial service on Sunday, June 21. Those who overindulged on dime-store mystery novels were quick to point out that this made Martin himself a suspect. After all, nobody seemed to recall Eleanor voicing a desire to be cremated after her death. When bodies are incinerated and reduced to ash, secrets tend to go up in smoke; there would be no way to examine them in the future, no way to exhume the corpses for future analysis. Could this have been a case of murder for hire? And could this explain the lone mysterious phone call Martin had made during his period of isolation?

Chief Deputy Coroner James Davidson attempted to put the murder theory to rest by announcing that the official photographs taken by the coroner clearly showed Eleanor's hand twined around the hammer that had been used as a lever in the rope which garroted her to death. This announcement sparked intense debate, as law enforcement had previously stated that the hammer in question was found under Eleanor's body, not in her hand. Some even went so far as to allege that the coroner's office had staged the death scene photos in order to bring the case to a close. Wouldn't suicide be the most convenient conclusion for detectives?

On Sunday, June 21, a conference was held between investigators and other parties and agencies involved in the case. The goal was to reach a consensus, and the meeting was adjourned after it was agreed that their "official" position was that Eleanor Feely had taken her own life after murdering her children in a fit of temporary insanity. This was based upon one irrefutable fact—not a single piece of hard evidence pointing to murder from an outside party had been uncovered. Conversely, they had been able to recreate a possible scenario supporting the murder-suicide theory:

Eleanor, her nerves and mind strained from nursing her sick son back to health, prepared Janice for bed and noticed that she was feverish. Bobby's illness had led her to the brink of a nervous breakdown, and the thought of nursing another child back from scarlet fever set her over the edge. She went to the pantry drawer and retrieved a piece of twine which had come into the house around a package from the drugstore. She used half of the twine to strangle Janice but was interrupted by Bobby, who entered the room. She struck him on the head with the hammer before strangling him with the cord of his bathrobe. Next, she stabbed them with the ice pick before stabbing herself, first in the chest and then in the temple. Realizing these wounds were only superficial, she took the remaining twine and tied one end to the radiator pipe and the other around her neck. Twisting the twine around the handle of the hammer like a tourniquet, she finally strangled herself. Upon reenacting this possible scenario, investigators admitted that it would be awkward to carry out these actions with the right hand but not impossible.

Another interesting fact which emerged from this conference was the supposed "sailor's knot," which some claimed would not have been used by a woman. Police determined that a sweater which Eleanor had been knitting for Bobby at the time of their deaths used the very same type of knot. While this fact bolsters the suicide theory, it also presents an intriguing possibility. If Eleanor wasn't the killer, then perhaps it was a person who also knew how to knit. This might suggest a female killer and a female very close to the Feely family. This would explain why the landlord's dog didn't bark, why none of the neighbors heard a commotion, or why none of the victims put up a struggle. Might the motive have been jealousy?

Following the conference, after just three days of investigation, police announced that they were dropping their probe into the Feely murders. Mayor McNair, incidentally, did not participate in this conference; he resigned on a whim in October and was never again elected to office. However, he did not give up on his mission to solve the Feely triple-murder mystery.

FEELY SENDS FOR REINFORCEMENT FROM THE BIG APPLE
On June 24, two New York private investigators arrived at the Webster Hall Hotel, checking in under the names J. S. Harrellbrook and James O'Connell. Per the request of Martin Feely, the pair was conducting an independent investigation. Harrellbrook was a retired New York City homicide detective, and O'Connell was a criminology student. After conferring with Inspector Howard Forner and Detective Samuel Wheeler, the two private investigators went to Point Breeze to go over the Feely apartment. Inside, they found a previously undiscovered bloodstain on

THE ROOM OF DEATH . . . TRAGIC SCENE THAT GREETED POLICE WHEN THEY ENTERED Graphic artist's sketch showing the stark details of the Feely tragedy. Mrs. Eleanor Feely is on the floor of the apartment with a noose around her neck, the ends twisted around the radiator. In her crib, is the baby, Janice, 3, while on his cot is the little boy, Bobby, 5, both dead.

Pittsburgh Sun-Telegraph, June 19, 1936.

the floor, located about twenty-two inches from where Eleanor had been tied to the radiator pipe. The men were baffled, theorizing that the blood may have been smeared when Eleanor's body was moved.

While this new clue didn't answer any questions, it was sufficient to force Coroner McGregor to take another look at the case. On June 25, the coroner held a long closed-door conference at the morgue with Detective Wheeler while several chief figures in the case waited outside to be interviewed. These included the two New York private investigators, Martin Feely, Charles Young, John Dambach, Grace Stansbury, City Detective George Brubach, and Chief Deputy Coroner Davidson. A short time later, three more city detectives arrived, one of them bringing a paper bag containing three ice picks. Nurse Stansbury was the first witness called into the room, and it was reported by the Pittsburgh papers that she left the building in tears when the twenty-minute interview was over.

What took place during this round of questioning was never revealed, but it was reported that Martin hired a Washington, DC-based research criminologist named B. J. Creel to question several of Eleanor's friends, including Stansbury, the following day at police headquarters. Stansbury repeated her previous statement that Eleanor had exhibited signs of anxiety and suffered lapses of memory. This statement was refuted by Mrs. Austin Grupe, who was the last person to see Eleanor and her children alive.

"Mrs. Feely was not nervous," Grupe said to Creel. "She was relaxed from the strain of Bobby's illness and was in good spirits. It was the first serious illness of any of her children and if she was worried at any time I think it was only natural."

When the grilling was over, Martin said to reporters who had gathered outside the police headquarters, "Every day I'm more and more convinced that my wife did not kill herself and the children." The three private investigators hired by Martin expressed the same belief.

MONAGHAN TAKES OVER

Meanwhile, detectives were busily sorting through the slush pile of tips and leads from concerned citizens and anonymous sources. One city detective, Stuart Dapp, had been told by a female neighbor that she had heard Eleanor remark that screen doors of the apartment were kept locked because she was "afraid of a man in the neighborhood." The renewed investigation was placed in the capable hands of Walter Monaghan. Monaghan, who had cracked the case of the Martha Westwood murder one year earlier, was widely considered to possess the most brilliant crime-solving mind in Pittsburgh, earning him the reputation as an ace detective. There were striking parallels in the two cases; Martha, the wife of a McKees Rocks justice of the peace, had been shot three times in her bed while her children were sleeping and her husband was away from home. Much like the landlord's dog, Toots, the Westwood family's bulldog did not bark when the intruder entered the home. Monaghan concluded that the killer could only have been the husband, Justice of the Peace James Westwood, even though he seemingly had an airtight alibi. Monaghan was able to bust this alibi to pieces in his court-room testimony, and Westwood was convicted.

Martin appeared delighted over Monaghan's entrance, lauding him as the ablest sleuth in the city. Most importantly, there was now a source of centralized authority in the case. Sure enough, the ace detective was able to produce quick results. On August 13, it was reported that the City Detective Bureau had officially reversed its opinion, moving the case out of the "closed" classification and onto the list of unsolved murders. This reversal was based on blood tests performed by the US Department of Justice.

The Department analyzed bloodstains from the sheets of the daybed in which Bobby had been strangled and stabbed in the temple with an ice pick and found two distinct blood types—one matching the blood type of Eleanor, the other matching Bobby's blood type. According to the City Detective Bureau, this was proof that Eleanor had been stabbed on the daybed. But was it possible that Eleanor could've attempted suicide on the bed with an ice pick before strangling Bobby and herself?

City Detective Samuel E. Wheeler didn't think so. Wheeler, who had been quietly investigating the case ever since Mayor McNair had assigned it to him, believed that Eleanor's ice pick wound, though not fatal, was serious enough to render her unconscious. Wheeler stated that Mrs. Feely could not have risen from the bed, dragged herself over to the radiator, and twisted the tourniquet around her neck in her weakened state. She could not have carried the ice pick with her, said Wheeler, though it was found beside her body.

THE CASE OF THE MISSING TOWEL

This was one of the four "physical impossibilities" cited by the City Detective Bureau in its decision to reclassify the case as murder. The other three were: There were no fingerprints on the hammer, other than one careless detective's thumbprint; Eleanor's clothing was not disarranged in a manner suggesting self-strangulation; and there wasn't enough space near Eleanor's body for her to use the hammer as a lever for twisting the tourniquet. "She would've had to climb up on the radiator and hang head-down and twist the rope," stated Wheeler. "I tried until my elbows were raw from bracing myself on the floor. I couldn't do it, and I don't think Mrs. Feely hung head down from the radiator to commit suicide. . . . If this is murder, it's a cinch the killer was somebody well known to the family."

In mid-September, Detective Wheeler made a shocking announcement, claiming that a vital piece of evidence had mysteriously vanished. In one photo of the crime scene taken by the deputy coroner, a bloody towel was seen hanging over the edge of Janice's crib. This towel did not appear in the photos taken at the scene six hours later by police. So who took the towel, and why? Wheeler believed that the killer had returned to the apartment to steal the towel in order to make the murder-suicide angle seem more convincing. This could mean that Wheeler was right about the slayer being known to the Feely family, or it could also mean that a frustrated member of law enforcement removed the towel in order to bring the case to a simple and quick conclusion. Unfortunately, the missing towel is one of the many mysteries concerning the Feely murders.

While neither Wheeler nor Detective Monaghan ever directly accused Pittsburgh law enforcement of tampering with evidence, their statements concerning the handling of the case did not win them many friends within the department. When Wheeler turned in his report to Mayor McNair later that month, he charged officers with "a deficiency of proper police protection" of the crime scene, claiming that at least thirty curiosity-seeking civilians were inside the apartment when he first arrived. Wheeler wrote:

Close observation of the apartment revealed the rooms had been pretty well scrutinized by the curious public. Clothing had been distributed over the furniture and floors, furniture drawers ransacked, utensils generally handled, bed clothing thoroughly disarranged, in general illustrating a lack of proper police protection. Had they (the police) intelligently conformed to their duties it might have been possible to procure definite fingerprints or prominent clues.

Within days of receiving Wheeler's report, William McNair unexpectedly resigned as Pittsburgh mayor, citing an inability to work with city council. "He ended his term as mayor as he had conducted the city's affairs—abruptly, amazingly, and without warning of what was to come," stated the *Post-Gazette* on October 7. But while McNair had given up city politics, he didn't give up his crusade to solve the Feely murder mystery. *Detective Story Magazine* published McNair's account of the triple tragedy, resulting in a deluge of theories and suggestions from readers. One reader, a former New York City police officer, said that he was so shocked by McNair's story that he "got out of bed in the middle of the night" to pen his suggestions for solving the mystery.

THE CORONER'S JURY

Now that the case was getting national attention, the long-delayed inquest into the deaths of Eleanor, Janice, and Bobby Feely was finally set for Tuesday, November 24. Over thirty witnesses would be called upon to give their testimony before Coroner McGregor's six-man jury. In preparation for the inquest, Detective Wheeler requested a court order allowing him to use a lie detector to interrogate three of the witnesses who, according to Wheeler, knew more than what they had told authorities. The request was denied.

As many had predicted, the inquest proved to be a heated clash between two rival factions of law enforcement, with Detective Wheeler at the helm of the group of law enforcement officials who favored the murder theory and Detective George Brubach leading the argument for murder-suicide. Voices were raised, tables were pounded, and, after two days of testimony, Coroner McGregor's head was reeling. He called a recess until Friday, stretching the inquest to its third day and making it the longest inquest in Allegheny County history to that point.

The highlight of the inquest was the much-anticipated testimony of Bobby's nurse, Grace Stansbury. Stansbury once again declared that Eleanor Feely had been "exceptionally nervous and depressed," and jaws dropped when she testified that Eleanor had a death premonition. According to Stansbury, she had urged Eleanor not to give Bobby his birthday presents until Monday, when his scarlet fever quarantine was lifted. Eleanor supposedly replied, "Oh, just give him the presents now. I feel that there won't be any Monday." When questioned about the ice pick, Stansbury claimed that it had belonged to Eleanor. According to her testimony, she had been called to the Feely apartment to tend to Bobby when Eleanor brought out crushed ice to prepare a compress. When she asked Eleanor how the ice had been crushed, Eleanor told her she used the ice pick. However, when presented with a "line-up" of ice picks, she was unable to identify the one found next to Eleanor's body.

On Friday evening, a verdict was rendered. The coroner's jury decided that Eleanor Feely and her two children were murdered.

No arrests were ever made in the Feely case, and no suspects were detained or hauled in for questioning. The bodies of Eleanor and her children were cremated, the location of their ashes unknown. As for Martin Feely, he resigned from the faculty of the University of Pittsburgh the following year and moved to New York, where he accepted a position as chairman of the health education department at Abraham Lincoln High School in Brooklyn. He never remarried and passed away in 1995 at the age of ninety-two.

2

The Skeletons of Oyster Paddy's Tavern

ALLEGHENY COUNTY

During the nineteenth century, a tavern situated at the corner of First Avenue and Stanwix Street (then known as Ferry Street) served as the secret hideout for some of Pittsburgh's most dangerous criminals. Shortly before the owner, Hugh O'Donnell—locally known as "Oyster Paddy"— passed away in 1907, human remains were unearthed at the site of his notorious saloon during the construction of a new skyscraper. Since Oyster Paddy died taking his secrets to the grave, the fates and identities of these long-forgotten victims have never been ascertained, thereby forming the basis for one of the city's most perplexing unsolved mysteries.

On the morning of Friday, June 22, 1906, workmen employed by Howard Brothers Contractors were excavating a foundation for a new skyscraper when they uncovered a pair of human skeletons two feet beneath the kitchen of a derelict building which had once been Oyster Paddy's Tavern. Their initial supposition was that they had uncovered the remains of two Indians, but those old enough to remember the saloon and its infamous patrons during its heyday were highly skeptical of this explanation.

Back then, when taverns were largely unregulated, Paddy's regulars included some of the hardest, meanest men to ever haunt the Steel City waterfront. There was murderous Mike Burns, who would be killed by guards during a prison riot in Canada. There was Brocky McDonald, the bank robber who would eventually meet his demise at the hands of his own gang. There was Booby Adams, Blinky Morgan, Kid Munn, Dutch Tony, and an assortment of shady characters with colorful nicknames. The clientele consisted of gamblers, killers, safecrackers, and burglars whose exploits were known to detectives throughout the country. There was Joe Anderson, the bartender who operated his own crime syndicate when he wasn't pouring drinks for Oyster Paddy. All of them were dead now and could shed no light on the matter of the mystery skeletons. The only tavern regular who was still alive was Patsy McGraw, but he was locked up at Moundsville Penitentiary in West Virginia, doing hard time for his second murder conviction.

And, of course, there was Hugh O'Donnell. But the man everyone knew as Oyster Paddy was in no condition to talk. Feeble and stricken with inoperable cancer, the fifty-six-year-old spent most of his free time either at his brother's farm in Wexford or at the hospital in Wheeling, receiving treatment he hoped would stave off the Grim Reaper for a few more days.

Even when Paddy was young and vigorous, he never spent much time at his own establishment. It was Joe Anderson who called the shots, as well as poured them, and, according to those who frequented the dank watering hole, Anderson had a strict rule about snitching. Before the Brooks Law was passed in 1887, Oyster Paddy's regulars also included dozens of corrupt local politicians and policemen. But there was a code known to all who frequented the joint: It was understood that any secrets divulged by the patrons, no matter how incriminating, stayed within the confines of the tavern. Anderson himself saw to that. As a result, thugs and lawmen alike were free to brag about their exploits without fear of repercussion. This turned Paddy's into a sanctuary of sorts, a safe haven for hunters and the hunted alike.

THE KILLING OF TINY SLOAN
Despite Anderson's code, some of the activities which took place inside the tavern were so spectacular that word leaked out and spread throughout the city. The 1887 murder of William "Tiny" Sloan, which took place inside the tavern, is one such example.

NOTORIOUS OLD RESORT AND PLACE WHERE CLUES TO SUPPOSED TRAGEDY WERE FOUND

The Pittsburgh Press, June 23, 1906.

Sloan, who served as clerk to Chief of Police Nathan Brokaw, went into Oyster Paddy's at around three o'clock on the morning of August 22 with a petty thief named Sim King and two prostitutes who conducted their business under the names of Mame Hanley and Lulu Walters. Sloan, who was quite popular with the opposite sex, recognized a girl named Ida Miller, who was seated at a table with Patsy McGraw and Ed Tash. Sloan attempted to buy Ida a drink but was ordered to leave by McGraw, who was still harboring a grudge against the police for accusing him of an 1884 shooting and robbery inside a different bar. When Sloan asked why, Ida told him that McGraw had already given her a stern lecture about "talking to a copper."

"And just what do you mean by that?" demanded Sloan, offended that any of the tavern's patrons would regard him as a snitch.

"I meant just what I said!" sneered McGraw. "Besides, I have it in for you anyhow, you dirty, rotten sonuvabitch!" McGraw reached into his hip pocket and drew a revolver. Sloan warned McGraw that he better not try anything, but McGraw fired. The bullet struck Sloan in the abdomen. "I'm a goner," he moaned, falling backward and crashing against the bar. But when he saw that McGraw was preparing to take another shot, Sloan desperately lunged at the attacker. Oyster Paddy, who was behind the bar at the time, wrenched the weapon out of McGraw's hand, but the damage was done—Tiny Sloan's wound proved to be fatal, and he died six hours later at the Homeopathic Hospital.

The sound of the gunshot attracted Officer W. J. Onstott, who raced into the tavern. One of the patrons pointed out the shooter, and Onstott pointed his revolver at McGraw. Paddy, fearing for his friend's life, rushed at the officer and knocked the gun away. "That's not the man you want," lied Paddy. Onstott turned toward the proprietor and quietly warned him that if he tried a stunt like that again, he would end up with a lead ball in the belly, just like Tiny Sloan.

Once Chief of Police Brokaw learned that his clerk had been shot, he immediately ordered the arrest of everyone inside the tavern. Policemen swarmed Oyster Paddy's and hauled the patrons to Central Station. Patsy McGraw was eventually tried, convicted, and sentenced to a relatively short term in the Western Penitentiary. McGraw escaped from prison and was later recaptured in Kansas City, where he served out the remainder of his sentence. After his release, he moved to West Virginia, where his gun claimed another victim, and he paid for his crime with a life sentence at Moundsville.

THE LIFE AND TIMES OF OYSTER PADDY

Hugh O'Donnell earned his nickname as a young man working in "Dad" Heinley's seafood restaurant on Fifth Avenue as an oyster opener. Records indicate that Heinley's restaurant stood on the site of the Farmers Bank Building, which was a Pittsburgh landmark until its demolition in May of 1997. Sometime around 1875, O'Donnell went into business for himself, opening a small saloon and restaurant at the corner of Ferry and Water Streets. Business thrived, eventually forcing him to open a larger establishment at First Avenue and Ferry Street. Not long afterward, Oyster Paddy's began to earn its unsavory reputation.

Oyster Paddy's Tavern at the corner of First Avenue and Ferry Street. The Wabash Bridge, a Pittsburgh landmark until its dismantling in 1948, is in the background. *The Pittsburgh Press*, June 23, 1906.

Then, in May of 1887, came the Brooks High License Law, which eventually put O'Donnell out of business. The "Brooks Law" created a strict statewide licensing system and required bar owners to pay exorbitant fees in order to obtain a license to sell "spiritous, vinous, malt and brewed liquors." The cost of the license was based on the population of the city in which the establishment was located, which, in Pittsburgh, amounted to five hundred dollars. This was no small sum in those days and is the equivalent of roughly $16,200 in today's currency. While the Brooks Law was intended to reduce unlawful behavior, it had the opposite effect. Many saloon owners preferred to take the risk of operating illegally. If caught, their fine would pale in comparison to the cost of a license. Ironically, it was during this period when many of the city's bars came under ownership of underworld figures and career criminals. They were among the few who had the financial means to obtain a liquor license.

O'Donnell applied for a license just once, and his appearance before the court of quarter sessions was so disastrous that he never attempted it again. At the hearing, the judge, after reading O'Donnell's application, looked down from the bench and asked, "Aren't you the one they call Oyster Paddy?"

"Yes, sir," replied O'Donnell.

"I am surprised that you would ask this court for a license at all," growled the judge. "That is all."

And so ended Oyster Paddy's business career—at least in Pennsylvania.

O'Donnell left Pittsburgh and went to the thriving oil boomtown of Sistersville, West Virginia, where he attempted to open another restaurant but failed. He then planned to open a restaurant in Johnstown, but his plans were derailed by the legendary flood of 1889. His money spent, O'Donnell was forced to take a low-paying job at a lunch counter in Wheeling, where he lived for the remainder of his life. The man known to a generation of rivermen and rulebreakers as Oyster Paddy passed away on Sunday, April 14, 1907, while on a train. He had just been discharged from a hospital in Wheeling and was on his way to Wexford, where he hoped to pass away surrounded by family. His brother, William, was with him at the time of his death.

The Reluctant Coroner

O'Donnell was quietly dying in a West Virginia hospital when workmen discovered the skeletons beneath the infamous tavern that once bore his name. Coroner Joseph G. Armstrong refused to investigate the matter until police presented him with some solid evidence suggesting foul play. As far as the coroner was concerned, the bones were those of forgotten Indians or early settlers who dwelled along the Monongahela during frontier times. Armstrong's heel-dragging not only hindered the investigation but may have also sabotaged it entirely. According to Chief Deputy Harry Lowe, curiosity seekers had stolen several of the bones from the work site by the following day. John F. Lally, the detective who first examined the skeletons, concluded that some corrosive chemical—perhaps lye or quicklime—had been used to hasten the decomposition process. He based this conclusion on the condition of a cheap, silver-colored pocket watch found alongside one of the skeletons, the metal appearing to have been exposed to some sort of acid. Yet, despite the detective's conclusion (and the fact that Indians didn't possess pocket watches), Armstrong adamantly refused to impanel a coroner's jury.

As was to be expected, wild rumors began to circulate along the Pittsburgh waterfront. Since the pocket watch was found in a battered, crushed condition with the hands of the timepiece eternally fixed at eight o'clock, many believed that the victim had been killed elsewhere and taken to Oyster Paddy's for a hasty burial under the cover of darkness, after the establishment had closed for the evening. This seemed plausible, since the tavern would have been packed with patrons at eight o'clock and the murder of two persons certainly could not have been carried out in secrecy, even with Joe Anderson's strict code of silence.

Others claimed that the bones were those of two detectives who had broken the tavern's anti-snitching policy, but Roger O'Mara, a retired Chief of Detectives, squelched this rumor. No city detectives had gone missing during his lengthy tenure. Strangely enough, O'Mara had nothing but praise for Oyster Paddy, calling him a "good fellow" who was no worse than any other bar owner in the city (the judge who denied him a liquor license in 1887 probably would've expressed a different opinion, however). "The resort of Oyster Paddy was no worse than many others," O'Mara stated, "but it was by the river and, therefore, patronized to a great extent by river men. The most desperate criminals, however, did not congregate there. They took to the hotels, where they had more privacy to concoct their schemes."

THE BLINKY MORGAN GANG

History refutes O'Mara's claims, of course. Many nefarious schemes and plots were hatched inside Oyster Paddy's, such as the infamous 1887 robbery of the Benedict and Ruedy Fur Store in Cleveland carried out by the Blinky Morgan gang, which used the tavern as its headquarters. Blinky's gang stole $15,000 worth of furs and brought them back to Pittsburgh to sell on the streets, which subsequently resulted in Kid Munn's arrest. Authorities attempted to transport Munn back to Cleveland, but Blinky and the rest of his gang ambushed them outside of Ravenna, Ohio, resulting in the death of one of the officers. Blinky Morgan was executed in Columbus for the officer's murder.

Oyster Paddy's was also the place where the spectacular and successful plot to crack the safe of the Pennsylvania Railroad Depot at Third Street and Liberty Avenue was hatched. After the robbery, the bandits hurried back to the tavern to hide from the police, knowing their secret would be safe with the patrons. Even Roger O'Mara's favorite informant, identified in papers only as a "Negro stool pigeon," was slashed to ribbons inside Oyster Paddy's tavern.

Sol Coulson, a twenty-nine-year veteran of the city police force, agreed with O'Mara's assertion that the skeletons found by workers could not possibly be those of missing policemen or detectives. If two law enforcement officials had gone missing, Coulson would have certainly known about it.

Superintendent Thomas A. McQuaide offered his own theory, insisting the murders had been carried out sometime after Hugh O'Donnell closed the tavern and moved to West Virginia. Newspaper reporters combed their archives trying to dig up stories of unsolved murders and missing persons from the previous three decades, but they couldn't find any puzzle pieces that fit.

A POSSIBLE SUSPECT

The rumor that gained the most traction, and by far the most plausible explanation, was that the killings were carried out by bartender Joe Anderson, who ruled the tavern with an iron fist whenever O'Donnell left town on one of his frequent trips. Is it possible the skeletons belonged to a pair of gangsters or thieves who made the mistake of double-crossing Anderson?

Anderson was known to be the ringleader of his own band of burglars. These bandits entered the tavern through a back door to divvy up their spoils, under Anderson's supervision. These facts seem to suggest the murdered men may have been members of Anderson's gang who, upon

The infamous Irish mobster Blinky Morgan (whose real name was Charles Conklin) was a regular customer at Oyster Paddy's. *The Cleveland Public Library Digital Gallery.*

returning from a successful robbery, got into an argument with Oyster Paddy's bartender and were given a swift and terrible reward for their efforts. But if Anderson played a role in burying the bodies beneath the kitchen floor, he never felt the icy breath of justice on his neck—at least not in the earthly realm. Anderson died ten years before the skeletons were discovered.

"I'm not surprised by anything they may find under the place," declared former Police Captain Charles Gallant to the Pittsburgh *Daily Post* after the skeletons were found. "It was no doubt the toughest resort in the United States at the time. But one thing can be said: Oyster never participated in any of the crimes which were planned there. The place seemed to be known to every thief in the country, and every one of them would go straight to the saloon as soon as he reached Pittsburgh." Gallant knew from experience that this was true; not only was he a former police captain, but he had also been one of Oyster's bartenders.

Of all the policemen who spent time inside the tavern—either drinking liquor or serving it—few were as intimately familiar with the rabble-rousers, rivermen, and roustabouts who made Oyster Paddy's their home away from home. In 1906, Gallant shared his own story about the infamous Blinky Morgan gang:

> One evening the whole gang, including Blinky Morgan and his bunch, were in the place when a riverman came in. Joe Baker took him outside and stole $40 from him. The riverman hunted up a gang of his friends and they came back. The battle that followed was a beaut—guns, knives, glasses, sandbags and paving stones were the weapons, and the gang almost tore up Ferry Street to get enough cobblestones. Oyster and I each got a baseball bat and finally drove everybody out of the place. Then we stood at the door, and when anybody stuck their head in it we soaked them with the bats. That was the only way to keep order in the place.

The former police captain and bartender added that, during his tenure at the saloon, he saw many strangers who had made the careless mistake of wandering inside, only to be led away from the building by thieves. "We never saw them again," explained Gallant. "There was a rumor in circulation that two fellows, suspected of being detectives, had been murdered by the gang, but that was before I went to work there."

Perhaps the primary reason why the mystery of Oyster Paddy's skeletons remains unsolved is because the authorities didn't know too little—they knew too much. Oyster Paddy's was a place where patrolmen and pickpockets sat side by side, where murderers and mayors went to unwind after dark, where politicians and prostitutes drank their worries away. Like Cheers, the fictional Boston bar, Oyster Paddy's was the sort of place where everybody knew your name.

3

The Hometown Flag Day Massacre

SCHUYLKILL COUNTY

During the 1930s, the Coal Region of Pennsylvania was a hotbed of mob activity. From Scranton to Shamokin, from Pittston to Pottsville and from Wilkes-Barre to Wiconisco, just about every bar, hotel, dance hall, and pool room was smudged with the fingerprints of cold-blooded gangsters. The "vice kings" of the era, such as Mount Carmel's infamous Louis Moff, padded their pockets bootlegging liquor and running illegal gambling parlors. Others, like Marie Nolan, dubbed "The Roadhouse Queen of Paxinos," pulled in big bucks operating brothels. From the famously seedy Sunset Inn in Numidia to the Bellevue Hotel in Kulpmont, these houses of ill repute were favorite hangouts where underworld types met to hatch their nefarious plots.

One establishment with a similarly shady past was the Rio Rita Inn, a raucous dance hall located in the borough of Hometown in Schuylkill County, on the "Old Tamaqua-Hazleton Highway" (present-day Lincoln Drive). This inn, formerly known as the Amber Lantern, was quite well known to prohibition agents during its heyday in the early 1930s, when the cabaret was under the ownership (at least on paper) of William Hurley of Pottsville. Despite numerous raids, locals and out-of-towners alike flocked to the Amber Lantern to dine and dance. To illustrate the type of entertainment offered, Amber Lantern advertisements of the era featured acts such as Madge Locke and the Sunkist Beauties, Baby Iris, The Duncan Personality Girls, and fan dancer Lydia Satty.

Prohibition came to an end in December 1933, and so did the glory days of the Amber Lantern. In 1935, the Amber Lantern became the Rio Rita Inn (the name being either a reference to a 1927 Broadway musical of the same name, or a play on words for Rita Rio, who was a famous singer and dancer of the era). Owner Manny Sturial brought Rocky Caruso on board as manager. Under Caruso's management, prices were lowered and the quality of entertainment became more risqué. When Rio Rita's liquor license was revoked in 1936 due to the establishment's unsavory reputation, Sturial was prohibited from operating his nightclub for one year and was not permitted to obtain a license for three years. Sturial sold the Rio Rita to Dominic Daldoni and Lee Gilbert in February of 1937, and clean-cut Tamaqua restaurateur Eddie Raabe was brought in as manager later that year.

Though it finally appeared that the Rio Rita had shed its seedy image, things went downhill fast; by January of 1938, the property had been sold to Michael Barella, who made the decision to shut down the Rio Rita. However, neighbors often reported seeing cars parked outside the abandoned building, and it was widely gossiped that the building was being used as a secret meeting place for gangsters.

THE FLAG DAY MASSACRE

It was shortly after six o'clock on a Tuesday morning in June of 1938 when nearby residents were startled by a deluge of gunshots. Those who were looking out their windows before the shots rang out might've seen a car slowly cruising past the abandoned Rio Rita building with three young men inside. If they had waited a little longer, they would've seen the car return a short while later with an additional passenger inside. But it never would've crossed their minds that, of these four men, three would be dead within thirty minutes.

One such resident was Jacob Sheafer, who lived in a small house about fifty yards from the Rio Rita. At six o'clock, a blue Packard drove up the dirt road leading to his house. Believing that a confused motorist was attempting to turn around, Sheafer thought little of it at the time. The car drove off in the direction of Tamaqua but returned a few minutes later with an additional passenger.

It was around 6:30 in the morning when a family was eating breakfast at Amy's Tea Room and Coffee Shop about 150 yards down the highway from the Rio Rita. The owner, Amy Faust, was a demure, soft-spoken woman with a naturally nervous disposition, and so she was understandably startled when she looked out the window and saw a well-dressed man staggering toward the Tea Room. He opened the front door, stumbled past the candy counter, and dropped onto the floor. Faust, thinking the man was drunk, hadn't heard the gunshots, but when a pool of blood formed beneath the collapsed stranger it was evident that something was terribly wrong. The man attempted to speak but choked on his own blood. He died without revealing any information, while customers fled from the building in terror.

Faust gathered her wits and immediately notified the police. Sheriff Fred Holman and Schuylkill County Chief of Detectives Louis Buono raced to Hometown to investigate. They were soon joined by Patrolman Lester Lucas of the State Motor Police and Deputy Coroner Mary Jones. Detective Buono followed the trail of blood from the Tea Room to the rear of the abandoned Rio Rita Inn and noticed that the window of the dance hall had been broken. Buono had been summoned to the Rio Rita in the past to investigate various complaints by neighbors but couldn't remember if the window had always been broken. The door to the dance hall, however, was riddled with bullet holes. Buono pushed open the door and found the darkened dance hall splattered with blood, and he followed a long smear on the floor—evidence of a body being dragged—to the cloakroom. It was there he found the bodies of two men, carelessly heaped atop each other like bags of trash. One had been shot through the chest, head, and back. The other had been shot multiple times in the chest and face. Like the third victim, the men were dressed in expensive and fashionable clothing. Huge pools of blood were on the floor, but there appeared to be no evidence of a struggle.

It was evident to Detective Buono that the victims had been ambushed by surprise and that a sawed-off shotgun had been used. Though pistol shots had also been fired, only two had missed their target; one of the bullets was found embedded in a pillar in the middle of the dance hall, and the other, Buono believed, had broken the window.

Buono's theory was that the man who died on Amy Faust's Tea Room floor had been able to escape and was shot in the back through the wooden door with the shotgun as he fled the scene.

The circumstances were eerily similar to a shooting that took place at the Cornfield Inn not far from Hometown seven years earlier, when an unidentified gunman, believed to have been a mobster, walked into the inn and opened fire, killing a man and a woman. A boxing manager named Al Jeanetti, who co-owned the nearby Ringside Inn, was murdered in a Wilkes-Barre roadhouse by a mobster in 1933. The detective immediately recognized the pattern and determined that the massacre had been a mob killing.

IDENTIFYING THE VICTIMS

The two men inside the cloakroom were soon identified as thirty-seven-year-old Peter Biscotti and twenty-five-year-old Giustoni Starace. Both men were from Philadelphia, and both had extensive police records. Starace had been arrested six times on weapons charges and had been a suspect in an Atlantic City robbery but was never convicted. Biscotti had been arrested twice—once for a hit-and-run and once in connection with an armed robbery. Biscotti also had several different aliases, including "Little Petey Ford" and "Peter Fordano." After autopsies were performed (twelve bullets were found inside Biscotti, and nine were found in Starace, along with an abundance of buckshot), the bodies were claimed by relatives at the Griffith Funeral Home in Tamaqua and taken back to Philadelphia.

It was considerably more difficult to identify the man who had died in Mrs. Faust's Tea Room, however. Inside his pocket was found identification belonging to a Philadelphia man by the name of Leonard Adducci, but investigation revealed that Adducci was alive and well and working in Perth Amboy, New Jersey. A relative of the victim soon arrived in Tamaqua and identified the body as that of his brother, Leonard Pugliese, also of Philadelphia. Pugliese's identity was also confirmed by several residents of nearby Hazleton, who claimed that the victim had arrived there three weeks earlier and had ruffled the feathers of local gangsters by attempting to elbow in on the numbers racket.

Where Triple Gangster Slaying Took Place

The roadhouse where the massacre took place (top), and Amy's Tea Room and Coffee Shop (below) where Peter Pugliese died. Allentown *Morning Call*, June 15, 1939.

Interestingly, none of the relatives who came forward to claim the bodies showed any emotion at the sight of their slain family members. There was no weeping, no outward signs of grief. Even more interestingly, all three relatives listed the occupation of their deceased "family members" as tailors. While the three victims were fashionably dressed, all of them wore off-the-rack ready-made suits, not tailored ones.

TERROR BEHIND THE PIANO

There was no evidence found outside the Rio Rita suggesting that the victims had been killed elsewhere and their bodies carried into the building. Based on evidence found at the scene and statements given by neighbors, the prevailing theory was that the three victims had been lured to the derelict dance hall, unaware of the assassins waiting inside. If the three men seen in the car that morning had first gone to the Rio Rita, it stands to reason that two of those three men were the killers. They went inside and prepared for the ambush. The car (with the same driver) then returned a short time later with the three victims, thereby explaining why the car, when seen for the second time, had gained an extra passenger. The victims, it was believed, had left their own car parked somewhere in

Gang Massacre Victims

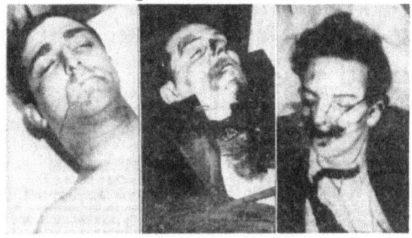

Victims of yesterday morning's gangland massacre near Tamaqua are shown above. Left to right they are Leonard Pugliese, 31, an unemployed pants maker of Philadelphia, who first was thought to be Leonard Adducci of Philadelphia; Giustino Starace, 37, of Philadelphia, one of the victims found in the check room of the "Amber Lantern," and Peter (Little Petey Ford) Bisciotti, also of Philadelphia, the second victim whose body was found in the check room.

Allentown *Morning Call*, June 15, 1938.

the vicinity. After the massacre was complete, the driver and the gunmen abandoned their vehicle and took the victims' automobile. Had Leonard Pugliese not escaped from the dance hall and tumbled into the tea room, there's a very good chance that the bodies would not have been discovered for several days, if not weeks.

On Wednesday morning, June 15, authorities reconstructed the crime scene. Based on their reenactment, it would appear that the gunmen had hidden behind the piano in the dance hall and had ambushed their victims from behind with sawed-off shotguns when they reached the center of the dance floor. Leonard Pugliese was able to run away before being shot in the back and neck. After Giustoni Starace and Peter Biscotti had fallen, they were fired upon at close range with pistols. That same day, police also found the abandoned blue Packard sedan nine miles away in Mahanoy City. The vehicle was registered to a Philadelphia restaurant owner named William Santore. In the backseat were found bloodstained papers.

Two residents of North Main Street in Mahanoy City told reporters that a man had parked the car around 6:45 on Monday morning, just fifteen minutes after the shooting. The only reason they noticed this particular car was because its driver had scraped the fender of another vehicle while parking. They described the driver as a "dark and swarthy" male wearing a checkered coat. This man walked away from the vehicle and hadn't been seen since. It was soon learned that a vehicle with the same plates was being sought in Baltimore, where a tavern had been bombed a day before the Rio Rita murders. The plates, "937-M," were registered to Giustoni Starace.

In Philadelphia, police were confident that the killers would soon be caught. "We're making satisfactory progress and I feel we will find the solution before the day is over," stated Captain James Ryan on Thursday. By this time, Philadelphia police had already arrested and released William Santore. In Tamaqua, two local business owners were hauled in for questioning. Michael Barella, who owned the dance hall at the time of the murders, was also arrested and released after questioning. Slowly but surely, the joint efforts of local, state, and Philadelphia police were gleaning valuable information.

Scarface Pete and Jimmy the Sheik

On June 24, the operator of a pool hall in nearby Shenandoah was committed to the Schuylkill County Prison, charged with three murders. Joseph Spigo, alias Joseph Jackman/Joe DiGiacomo, was arrested after a man from Barnesville, Edward Saroka, came forward stating that he saw the blue Packard on the morning of the massacre and recognized the driver as the man he knew as Joseph Jackman. Spigo would later post bail.

Less than a month later, the case would be turned on its head with the discovery of a body Detective Louis Buono believed to be a fourth victim of the Flag Day Massacre. On Tuesday, July 12, the badly decomposed body of a man was found at the bottom of a bootleg "coal hole" a quarter mile south of Delano. A hole in the chest suggested the man had been stabbed to death. The body was identified as forty-one-year-old Wilkes-Barre barber Peter Gallelli. Like most folks with mafia connections, Gallelli also had a variety of colorful aliases, including "Pete the Slash," "Scarface Pete," Pete Gallo, and Peter Russelli.

Gallelli was a known accomplice of the three slain mobsters and had an extensive rap sheet in Buffalo and Brooklyn. He had mysteriously vanished around the same time as the murders but was not killed the same day, as witnesses later saw him at the Griffiths undertaking parlor in Tamaqua viewing the bodies. "It's too bad they were killed," Gallelli had said to the undertaker's wife. "I don't know them, but they look like nice fellows to me." That was the last time Gallelli was seen alive.

Like the other big city mobsters involved in the case, Gallelli had come to the Anthracite Region less than a year earlier, settling first in Shamokin and then Wilkes-Barre, where he operated a barbershop. It was a colleague who identified his remains through a shoe, belt buckle, watch, and other personal effects found on the badly decomposed body. This led authorities to believe that Gallelli was either killed by local mobsters for being the "contact man" of the Philadelphians or had been killed by the Philadelphians for being an informant to the local mobsters. Police admitted that, because of the poor condition of the body, an arrest was unlikely. Gallelli was promptly buried at Union Cemetery in Schuylkill Haven.

Months passed without a break in the case, but things took a stunning turn on November 28 when a man walked into the office of a former Schuylkill County judge claiming to be one of the men responsible for the Flag Day Massacre. The man was thirty-seven-year-old bootlegger James Amato, better known around the Coal Region as "Jimmy the Sheik." Amato was the alleged ringleader of an illegal liquor plant in Northumberland County and was awaiting sentencing in federal court when he walked into the law offices of Roy P. Hicks and asked the former judge to represent him after he turned himself in for his role in the Hometown slayings.

Accompanied by Hicks, Amato entered the office of District Attorney Clarence A. Whitehouse in Pottsville later that day and surrendered himself. An hour later, he was arraigned before Tamaqua magistrate A. R. Snyder on a charge of murder. After being fingerprinted at the State Motor Police barracks, Amato was taken to the county jail. That afternoon, Judge Palmer set bail at $7,500. Although Amato posted bail, he was sentenced a short time later for the Northumberland County liquor charge. By the time of his release from prison in December of 1939, no other arrests had been made in the Flag Day Massacre. The next arrest came in January of 1940, when thirty-year-old Anthony Porelli of Philadelphia was held without bail in connection to the Hometown massacre.

A SUSPICIOUS FIRE AND A DISINTERESTED PROSECUTOR

Things took another strange turn on the afternoon of August 15, 1940, when the derelict dance hall, now owned by Thomas Greiner, was gutted by flames. Much of the building was completely destroyed, along with any overlooked evidence that may have been inside. Firefighters from the Park Crest Hose Company and the American Hose Company from Tamaqua made a valiant attempt to stop the flames from spreading to the adjoining structure occupied by Joseph Calabrese. Strangely, the roof of Calabrese's home caught fire later that night (presumably from drifting embers from the earlier fire). The cause of the fire has never been determined.

Interior of the Rio Rita. The arched doorway leads to the cloakroom, where the bodies of Peter Biscotti and Giustoni Starace were found. Peter Pugliese attempted to escape through the door to the left of the cloakroom. Allentown *Morning Call*, June 15, 1938.

As the year progressed with no further developments in the Hometown murders (Amato and Spigo were still out on bail with no trial date in sight), the public began to turn on District Attorney Whitehouse, who seemed to have more of an interest in his own re-election than the pursuit of justice. When asked why the suspects had yet to be prosecuted, the district attorney flippantly replied, "That's the work of the State Police." As the November elections drew near, several papers pointed out that the number of unsolved murders during Whitehouse's tenure was piling up and that he had not secured a single murder conviction during his term in office. When pressed on this topic, Whitehouse intimated that, since he had inherited these cases from his predecessor, he was not responsible for prosecuting them. This caused the Mahanoy City Record American to remark: The record of what the District Attorney has not done is more voluminous than what he has done.

Despite these criticisms, Whitehouse succeeded in winning re-election and continued to serve as district attorney until 1950. By this time, the murder charges had been dropped against Amato and Spigo by the district attorney's office, since Whitehouse had no desire to prosecute the suspects. Though one of the suspects had turned himself in to authorities, neither James Amato nor Joseph Spigo or Anthony Porelli ever stood trial in the Rio Rita murders, which still remain unsolved.

Sadly, it seems that Whitehouse's preoccupation with his own political ambitions was a significant factor in why the killers behind the Flag Day Massacre were never caught or brought to justice. Quite simply, it appeared that Clarence Asa Whitehouse wanted to follow in the footsteps of his father and grandfather. His grandfather, W. John Whitehouse, was a Schuylkill County District Attorney, delegate for four Republican National Conventions, and once sought the Republican gubernatorial nomination. His father, a Princeton graduate, had also served as Schuylkill County District Attorney before being elected to the House of Representatives. He then became a judge but died of a heart attack at the age of forty-seven.

And like his father, Clarence A. Whitehouse Jr. was also a Princeton graduate with a long tenure as district attorney. In 1950, he was appointed Deputy State Attorney General, a position he held for five years. And, also like his father, Whitehouse died prematurely from heart disease. While vacationing in Rhode Island in 1960, he suffered a fatal heart attack on a luxury cruise and died at the age of fifty-three. Though his legacy was lauded by Schuylkill County newspapers after his death, to the residents of Hometown, he left a stain that has never washed away.

The old roadhouse once known as the Amber Lantern and the Rio Rita was eventually rebuilt and is currently a private residence. In 1991, the building was bought by Joseph Durham, a Kansas resident who had moved to Hometown. The *Pottsville Republican* noted in 1995 that Durham had no idea about the building's lurid past when he purchased it. Despite its bloody history, Durham told the Republican that he loved the house and the neighborhood, and he added that, no, he had never experienced any hauntings or paranormal activity. "I'm not superstitious," he added.

4

The Hershey Torch Murder

DAUPHIN COUNTY

The unique 1928 case of the Hershey Torch Murder, as it was dubbed by the media, baffled State Police for two years before the guilty person, Charles Kaldes, was arrested and convicted. Now, you may ask yourself, "If Kaldes was convicted, how can this be considered an unsolved murder?" Therein lies the bizarre wrinkle in this strange case. You see, this was the rarest type of murder investigation—the type in which it is the victim, and not the killer, whose identity is unknown. For that matter, it is unclear whether Kaldes ever murdered anyone; the crime to which he pleaded guilty was insurance fraud.

On the Sunday morning of September 23, 1928, Marvin Kieffer was driving home from his job at the airport in Middletown. Along Union Deposit Road, just outside of Hershey, he saw a car at the bottom of an embankment that was engulfed in flames. He then saw a sight that must've been truly horrifying: the outline of a human body inside the inferno. Although he knew that he was too late to save the life of the victim, he parked on the shoulder and then ran toward the blazing two-door coupe, but the heat was too intense. He watched helplessly as the flames consumed the occupant, who had made no attempt to escape.

"All of the windows of the car were closed," Kieffer stated. "By the time I got to the car, the fire had spread to the rear inside and the flames were shooting fifteen feet in the air. I saw a man sitting on the floor behind the front seat. His back was resting on the left side of the car. I

43

saw (that) his face and hair were burning. I believe he was dead because he made no effort to move." The only movement inside the vehicle was the jerking of the victim's hand, which the Dauphin County coroner later attributed to the rapid shrinking of muscle tissue from the fire's intense heat.

Within moments, two young motorists from York pulled over to assist Kieffer. When they, too, realized that it was too late to save the victim's life, Kieffer drove them to the Hershey Men's Club, where they sent in a fire alarm. Firemen from the Hershey Fire Company soon extinguished the blaze, but the remains of the victim were charred beyond recognition. Lieutenant Pickering of the State Highway Patrol soon arrived on the scene and, after a brief examination, turned the case over to the State Police. Meanwhile, Coroner J. H. Kreider was notified.

Coroner Kreider was unable to find any clue that could aid police in identifying the victim. An arm and a leg had been burned off completely, and other parts were so thoroughly charred that he couldn't ascertain the cause of death, though he discovered that the skull had been fractured in two places, while a hole, about three inches in diameter, was found on the left side of the skull. Whether the fractures were the result of the fire, an accident, or foul play, the coroner couldn't be certain, but State Police were confident they were dealing with a case of murder. They believed the victim had been dealt several blows on the side of the head before being placed in the automobile, which was then doused with gasoline, set on fire, and pushed down the embankment to give the illusion of an accident.

Authorities soon discovered the car's license plates had been issued to Charles Kaldes of 406 Briggs Street, Harrisburg. Kaldes was not unknown to authorities; County Detective John Yontz knew that the twenty-seven-year-old man was a small-time criminal and had been involved with a gang of bootleggers. In Harrisburg, Kaldes rented a room from W. C. Toomey and his wife, and Toomey told reporters that Detective Yontz had instructed them not to discuss the case. According to Toomey, there was something about the case that was "dangerous to disclose to newspapers." Toomey would only reveal that Kaldes had lived in Harrisburg for just two weeks and that he was frequently away from home for several days at a time. Kaldes never spoke about where he was going or what he was doing. County and state officials also refused to divulge any details about Kaldes to the press.

A CANDYMAN TAKEN FOR A RIDE

Within a few days, State Police had developed a working theory. By now, it had been reported that a set of keys, belonging to Kaldes, had been found inside the pockets of the burned body and that Kaldes had been bootlegging liquor. During a search of his Briggs Street room, police found a letter referring to liquor deliveries in Lebanon County. In addition, several smashed bottles of liquor had been found inside the car. Kaldes had previously lived in Reading and Hamburg, and police believed that Kaldes had been "taken for a ride" by a group of more powerful rivals who feared that Kaldes had been cutting into their profits. They cited the fact that there was no damage on the vehicle consistent with an accident—and if Charles Kaldes hadn't died accidentally, it stood to reason that it had to be murder.

To prove this theory, police combed Dauphin and Berks Counties for witnesses who could shed some light on Kaldes' shadowy life and shady pastimes. In Harrisburg, they learned from car dealer Paul McCarthy that he had sold a used car to Kaldes on September 5 for two hundred dollars. Kaldes, whom the dealer described as having good manners and a pleasing personality, had given McCarthy $80 as a deposit, even though he saw about four hundred dollars when Kaldes opened his wallet. He recalled that his customer was well-dressed, wearing an expensive ring and scarf. The rest of the purchase was financed through the Harrisburg Finance Company, and the first payment was due the day before the automobile was burned. Kaldes never made this payment.

According to the records of the Harrisburg Finance Company, Kaldes had given his occupation as that of a self-employed candymaker, and it was learned that he had previously been employed by Hamburg confectioner Peter Martin. Martin recalled that Kaldes wasn't exactly a steady worker during his period of employment, often quitting and then begging for his job back a short time later. "The longest period that he worked for me was four or five months," stated Martin.

Sergeant Hartman and Lieutenant Bennett of the State Police were assigned to the case, and they learned that Kaldes carried life insurance policies with the Penn Mutual and Union Central companies of Berks County with a combined value of $12,500. This amount would be valued at nearly $135,000 in today's currency. Both policies included a double indemnity clause in the event of accidental death or murder, which meant that someone stood to gain $25,000. Listed as the beneficiary was a cousin, Kostas Haldos, a barber from Reading. Haldos told police that his cousin's policies were to be transferred to Kaldes' fiancée after the wedding, though he did not recall the name of the girl. The $5,000 Penn Mutual policy had been purchased on July 3, while the $7,500 Union Central policy had been purchased on July 18. It was the cousin, Kostas Haldos, who had paid the premiums.

The possibility that the man found in the burning car was not Charles Kaldes did not occur to Sergeant Hartman or Lieutenant Bennett. However, it did occur to both insurance companies. Representatives for Penn Mutual and Union Central promised that they would launch their own investigation. Even if the man in the car turned out to be Kaldes, a spokesperson for Union Central said his firm had a perfectly good reason to contest the policy on the grounds of fraudulent statement; Union Central would not have issued the policies if they had known their client earned his money from bootlegging liquor instead of making candy.

Funeral for the Victim

On Friday, September 28, a man believed to be Charles Kaldes was buried in Hummelstown Cemetery, beneath a simple wooden slab inscribed "Unidentified." The funeral was paid for by Kostas Haldos, who returned to Reading after the funeral to aid the State Police in their efforts to solve the crime. The police, meanwhile, had turned their efforts to locating the missing fiancée. Although Kaldes' photograph had been plastered all over the newspapers, the woman had not come forward. This caused some to wonder if she, too, was involved in criminal activity.

While funeral preparations were being made, Coroner Kreider was tasked with issuing the death certificate, though he wasn't quite sure what to write. He eventually settled upon the following: This body, when found in a burned automobile on the Union Deposit road, three-quarters of mile north of the William Penn Highway, was charred beyond recognition, with a hole in the left temple. Cause of death and identification is being investigated.

By now, police had been able to pin down Kaldes' movements before his supposed death. Just after renting a room from W. C. Toomey on September 4, Kaldes took a trip to Hartford, Connecticut. As soon as he returned to Harrisburg, he set out for Pittsburgh. Each time, the newly purchased car was left in the garage, and Toomey told police that he believed Kaldes didn't know how to drive. The last time the Toomeys saw their lodger was Thursday, September 20. He left the Toomey house that morning after paying his rent, drawing from his pocket an immense roll of banknotes. Toomey told police that he had no doubt that Kaldes had been murdered. With the careless way he flashed his bankroll and his fondness for flashy clothes, it seemed like it was only a matter of time before someone bumped him off.

HOLES IN THE MURDER THEORY

Reporters soon began to have their doubts about the murder theory, especially after they learned that Charles Kaldes did not know how to drive. Newspapermen besieged the State Police with questions, but no answers were forthcoming. They wanted to know about the mysterious fiancée. Who was she? Why hadn't she showed up to the funeral? Was anyone trying to find her? Isn't she now the central figure in the case? Reporters also doubted the bootlegging claims. Didn't bootleggers tend to be expert drivers? How would rival bootleggers have known when and where Kaldes would pass with a carload of liquor?

In October, George L. Long of the Union Central Insurance Company filed a request for the disinterment of the body found inside the burning auto near Hershey. In his request to Coroner Kreider, Long stated that his company's investigation suggested that the man found inside the car might have been dead long before the fire was set or—even more shockingly—might have been a corpse that had been dug up from a cemetery or stolen from a morgue. If such was the case, Long argued, embalming chemicals should still be traceable in the body. As luck would

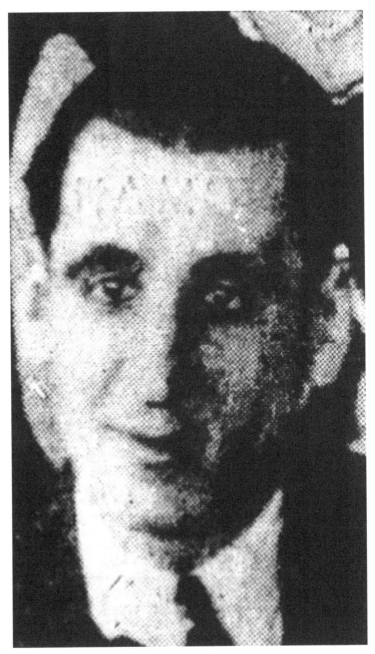

Charles Kaldes. Harrisburg *Telegraph*, June 13, 1930.

have it, the Hummelstown undertaker who prepared the charred remains, William Karmany, saw no point in embalming them, so the presence of embalming chemicals would prove that the body had been stolen for the purpose of insurance fraud. Now suspicion fell upon the Reading barber, Kostas Haldos. Haldos was held for three days and questioned at length but was able to clear his name.

THE GREEK WAITER'S STORY

The body at Hummelstown Cemetery did not need to be exhumed because a New York waiter named Nick Avronis came forward to tell police that Kostas Haldos had told him that he and his cousin had stolen it from a graveyard. Lieutenant Montgomery B. Bennett traveled to New York to question the waiter. Major Wilhelm, deputy superintendent of the State Police, said that he wasn't surprised by this turn of events; Haldos had abruptly left Reading in November, moving to New York without attempting to collect on his cousin's life insurance policy. He had taken a job as a waiter in a Greek restaurant on the Lower West Side. This seemed to suggest that Haldos fled because he was feeling the hot breath of justice on his neck.

This information was verified by both insurance companies, who said that Haldos had failed to present the final paperwork for the insurance payout. To collect on the policy, Haldos was required to present an affidavit certifying the death and burial of the policyholder. Since Coroner Kreider had made out the death certificate without listing Charles Kaldes' name—instead, he had written "Unidentified" on the document—Haldos was unable to present the required affidavit. It seems that while law enforcement was boldly predicting a bootlegging murder, Coroner Kreider was the first person who smelled a rat.

The State Police, on the other hand, refused to let go of their murder theory, pointing out that traces of blood had been found at the scene and that embalmed bodies can't bleed. Even the Penn Mutual Life Insurance Company had retracted their opinion that the body inside the car had been a stolen corpse.

It was the New York Police Department who first questioned Haldos about Avronis' story on March 30, 1929, but Haldos denied having made the incriminating statements. Haldos was hauled back to Harrisburg, along with Avronis and Peter Fisher (another waiter at the restaurant), who were held as material witnesses. Meanwhile, Sergeant Keller and Corporal Snyder of the State Police thoroughly searched Haldos' abandoned South Ninth Street apartment in Reading and uncovered damning evidence against him. Letters, photographs, and other personal property were examined at the West Reading barracks.

Lieutenant Montgomery B. Bennett openly stated he did not believe the story Haldos supposedly told to Avronis about the body being stolen from a graveyard. The police had explored this angle but could find no evidence of opened graves or missing bodies. Even if a dead body had been stolen, how did it end up with a gaping hole in the side of the skull? Why was there blood at the scene? Bennett was convinced more than ever that his murder theory was correct. In Harrisburg, it was hinted that District Attorney Robert T. Fox was preparing murder charges against Haldos and Kaldes, whom authorities believed was still alive and using an assumed name. In fact, Avronis and Fisher told the police they had seen Kaldes in New York, where he was employed in the check room of the Waldorf Astoria Hotel, going by the name of Kyriakos Karolidos.

By the following week, Kostas Haldos was being held at the Dauphin County jail without bail, following a hearing before Alderman William H. Charters. Also being held was Nick Avronis, whom Lieutenant Bennett accused of "tipping off" Kaldes after speaking to police on March 30, allowing him to flee. Lieutenant Bennett told reporters that Haldos and Kaldes had tried to obtain life insurance from eight other companies using a variety of aliases and that Haldos had a disturbing criminal record—a decade earlier, he had spent a year locked up in a Massachusetts prison for statutory rape.

THE BOSTON SUITCASE TRAP

After fleeing New York, Charles Kaldes sought refuge in Boston. This was the story given to Lieutenant Bennett by Nicholas Pappas, an acquaintance of the fugitive. Pappas, a former resident of Reading, had been arrested in Boston after Pennsylvania State Police, with the assistance of the Boston Police Department, laid an ingenious trap. While locked up in Dauphin County, Kostas Haldos wrote a letter to New York, requesting that his luggage be forwarded to a restaurant in Boston. This letter was intercepted by the NYPD and the information relayed to Lieutenant Bennett, who boarded the first train to Boston. There he planted a suitcase at the restaurant, expecting Kaldes to retrieve it. However, it was a man named Nicholas Pappas who showed up to claim the luggage. He was promptly arrested and extradited to Pennsylvania, where he was questioned about the Hershey Torch Murder. Within hours, District Attorney Fox formally charged the two cousins with "murder of an unidentified male" and insurance fraud.

A FAILED INDICTMENT

On June 1, District Attorney Fox failed to present the charge of murder against Kaldes and Haldos to the Dauphin County grand jury. Fox refused to discuss his action, adding that he had no statement for the press. Homer Kreider and Victor Braddock, attorneys for Kostas Haldos, threatened to file habeas corpus proceedings demanding the release of their client. According to the attorneys, there was no proof that Kaldes was alive or had been seen in New York. Charges were dropped, and Haldos was released from jail on June 4.

The search for Charles Kaldes, however, never stopped. "We'll get him," promised Lieutenant Bennett on September 23, 1929, the one-year anniversary of the Hershey Torch Murder.

CAUGHT AT LAST

On June 12, 1930, Charles Kaldes was captured by Detective Dolan of the New York Police Department. Lieutenant Bennett was tight-lipped about what charges, if any, would be brought against the long-sought fugitive. He immediately went to work lining up witnesses for the extradition hearing, which was to be held in New York. These included Ralph Hill of the Penn Mutual Insurance Company and George Zahner of the Union Central Insurance Company. Kaldes was handed over to the Pennsylvania State Police by Magistrate Michael Ford of the Third District Magisterial Court and left the courtroom in the custody of Bennett and Private Kerwin Jones. Both insurance men had little doubt about the New Yorker's identity. "There's no mistake about it," said Hill. "This is the fellow who applied for the policy. It is fortunate for us that the policies were so large, otherwise we should not have been suspicious and the investigation would not have been started."

Under a barrage of police questions, Kaldes admitted his guilt and claimed the body had been stolen from a graveyard by his cousin. Where or how he had obtained it, he couldn't say. Neither could he describe the body. "Ask Haldos," quipped Kaldes, perhaps unaware that his cousin had been re-arrested and extradited to Detroit, where he was once again convicted of statutory rape. This time, his sentence was far more severe than the one he had received in Boston.

Ultimately, Kaldes pleaded guilty to two counts of conspiracy to defraud an insurance company. In September, he was sentenced by Judge Hargest to two to four years of imprisonment—the maximum penalty under the law—in the Eastern Penitentiary. Homer Kreider, Kaldes' attorney, asked for leniency on the grounds that Haldos had conceived the plot and procured the body. The judge, however, was not convinced.

Even after both men were locked up, one in Detroit and the other in Philadelphia, police continued to search for clues to the identity of the man incinerated in the backseat of a two-door coupe on Union Deposit Road in 1928. A man who, by all accounts, still lies in an unmarked grave in Hummelstown. They checked every cemetery from Berks County to Dauphin County but never came across a grave that had been robbed. Some have speculated there may have been a third conspirator involved, perhaps a conspirator from a different part of the state, who had obtained the body. Still others insist that the body belonged to an unfortunate man who met his untimely demise at the hands of either Charles Kaldes or Kostas Haldos. This seems to be the most likely scenario, as evidenced by the blood found at the scene by police. And, to paraphrase Lieutenant Bennett, dead bodies don't bleed.

5

The Whittmore Case

It was ten minutes after nine in the morning and Rosemund Dunlap was running late. Her employer, the svelte and glamorous Doris Whittmore, would undoubtedly still be asleep in bed. Doris loved the nightlife, and hangovers on a Wednesday morning, or any other morning, for that matter, were not an infrequent occurrence. As Rosemund had anticipated, the front door to Ms. Whittmore's apartment was still locked. She fumbled for her key and let herself inside. As a maid, Rosemund wasn't paid to pry into the personal lives of her employers, but—like most domestic servants—she knew a few deep, dark secrets. The drab, brick house on Cherry Street was located in the heart of Harrisburg's "red light district," after all.

Sure enough, Doris Whittmore was still in bed, and, from the look of it, she must've had a pretty wild evening. The covers hadn't been turned down, and Doris was face-up on the mattress of her four-poster bed with her head beneath a pillow, clad in a revealing red evening gown that didn't leave much to the imagination. Her silk-stockinged legs were crossed and her shoes removed. Over the bed was an electric light with a long chain cord, the bulb missing. The maid studied Doris, and though the shabby but elegantly furnished room was steeped in morning gloom, she could tell that the thirty-year-old brunette wasn't breathing. She removed the pillow and screamed.

It was Rosemund's scream on September 30, 1931, which attracted a nearby policeman, who determined that Doris had been killed by a blow to the back of the head. A few drops of congealed blood were found on the sheets near the head. The room was tidy and did not appear to have been disturbed. The expensive diamond ring which Doris wore on her finger was still in place, and the watch on her wrist was still ticking. Twelve dollars in cash was found in a cedar chest in the bedroom. Robbery did not appear to be a motive. The police officer made a hasty search for the murder weapon but found nothing.

Within minutes, Harrisburg Chief of Police George J. Shoemaker was on the scene, accompanied by Captain Paul Schelhas, Dauphin County Detective John Yontz, and Coroner Milliken. The coroner estimated that the victim had been dead for about eight hours. The body was draped with a sheet and carried outside to a police patrol wagon bound for the hospital. A post-mortem examination revealed a fracture at the base of the skull. Detective Yontz questioned the maid in detail about her employer's habits and visitors, while the others searched the apartment for clues. The blinds had not been pulled down, and the window was locked from the inside. The furniture was in perfect order, except for a wooden chair with a broken back, and there were no signs of a struggle. Rosemund told police that she had broken the chair a week earlier while she was standing on it, trying to dust the blinds. Based upon the position of the body and the lack of blood, it was believed that Doris was already dead when placed onto the bed.

THE PRIVATE WORLD OF DORIS WHITTMORE

Rosemund Dunlap, along with neighbors and friends of the deceased, provided an interesting glimpse of Doris Whittmore's private life. Sally Magaro, a close friend who lived at the Wilson Hotel on the corner of Third and Cherry Streets, told police that Doris was a native of Vermont and had arrived in Harrisburg in February of 1931, after separating from her husband. She worked for a brief time as a waitress in Harrisburg. Sally last saw Doris around two o'clock the previous afternoon. "When I saw her, she seemed just the same as ever," said Sally. "I have no idea who could've done this."

"It's just too bad," said another neighbor. "She was a mighty nice girl and a good neighbor."

According to neighbors, Doris was very secretive. She spoke little about Vermont and even less about the man she'd left behind. In fact, no one seemed to know his name or whether he was living or dead. Doris had lived alone in her Cherry Street home since settling in Harrisburg but was known to entertain many male visitors. Doris was said to be a cheerful and well-dressed companion—at least for the right price—who loved dancing and drinking at local roadhouses. Frail in stature, the pretty brunette was five feet two inches in height and weighed not more than a hundred pounds. This made police wonder about suspects: Was she a casualty of war between elements of the criminal underworld, or was her death caused by a sudden blow to the back of a head by an angry lover? It was also possible that the killer had been somebody with an emotional attachment to Doris, as the pillow had been placed over the face by the perpetrator as though he (or she) did not want to look at it.

Acquaintances who frequented the Whittmore apartment were also interviewed by police. These included Thomas "Skeets" Pinto, George "Chooky" Magaro (Sally's husband), and Dominic "Clutch" DiPerna. While the origins of the nicknames of the first two men are a matter of conjecture, it was said that DiPerna earned his sobriquet because of a deformed arm and hand. Of these persons of interest, authorities were most interested in Pinto (whose real name was Michael Ciallela), who had been arrested a year earlier for operating a brothel on South Second Street. It was rumored that Pinto was suffering money troubles and had been receiving financial support from Doris at the time of her murder. When questioned about Whittmore, Pinto seemed excitable, nervous, and irritable. He also had a difficult time keeping his story straight when grilled by Detective Yontz; as a result, he was held at police headquarters for several days before his attorney procured his release. But, if Skeets Pinto thought that he was off the hook in the murder investigation, he was sorely mistaken.

ROBBED BY HER MAID

Mary Stine, the proprietor of a store near the intersection of Third and Cherry Streets, told police that she had sold Doris a pack of cigarettes around 8:30 the evening before the maid discovered the body. Doris was dolled up, as if going to a party. Aside from the killer or killers, it was possible that Stine was the last person to see Doris Whittmore alive.

On the night of the murder, two policemen had gone to the Whittmore home armed with a warrant issued by Alderman John P. Hallman, charging Doris with operating a "disorderly house." The policemen waited for several hours until midnight for Doris to return home, and the warrant was never served. This led authorities to believe that the murder occurred after the police officers had left. The officers claimed that no one had left or entered the home during the time they were keeping watch.

While robbery was not believed to be the motive, Sally Magaro told the *Harrisburg Telegraph* that Doris had been robbed of jewelry and cash totaling $1,000 in April, following a police raid of three houses of prostitution on Cherry Street that led to her arrest on a charge of immorality. The break-in occurred after Doris had been taken into custody. Her maid at the time, Almeda Morton, was arrested, along with another woman and two men she had let inside. The four defendants were later cleared by a Dauphin County grand jury. Doris, too, was cleared by a jury. According to Magaro, Doris never recovered emotionally from the incident (and it's probably safe to say that she didn't give Morton a good reference as a maid). It was shortly after this event when Doris began to associate heavily with tough "underworld" types—guys with colorful nicknames like Chooky, Skeets, and Clutch.

This incident was corroborated by Edith Bracken, one of the few female officers on the Harrisburg police force. Officer Bracken, along with Officer John Arnold, had accompanied Doris to her home after the robbery. Officer Bracken recalled that Doris was scared to go inside. "I'm always afraid of getting hit on the head every time I enter this place," Doris had said to Bracken. "Please don't make me go in there in the dark first."

Detectives believed that robbery would've been relatively simple, as Doris had a habit of greeting invited guests and strangers alike from

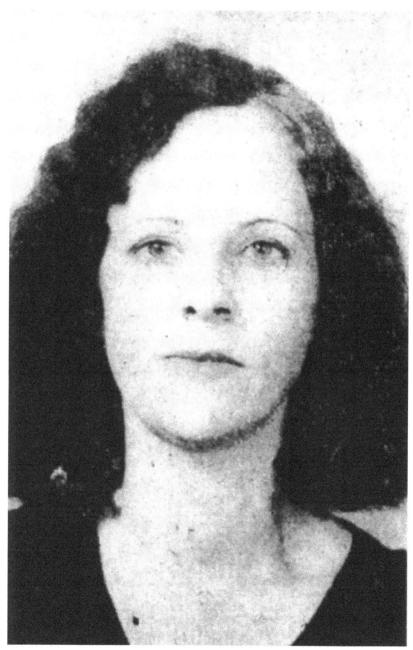

Doris Whittmore. *Harrisburg Telegraph*, September 30, 1931.

the window of her house, telling them to come inside. A robber could have entered the house without difficulty and departed without arousing suspicion. Since the coroner believed that Doris had died between the hours of one and three in the morning, robbery could not be ruled out completely. The robber might not have taken the ring because he didn't notice it on Doris' finger, or he may have been surprised by Doris while in the act. Twelve dollars had been left inside her cedar chest, but for all anyone knew, the box could've contained an untold sum of money. Of course, if robbery had been the motive, this would mean that Doris Whittmore had been killed inside her home, even though the condition of the apartment contradicted this theory.

Another possible motive was jealousy. According to friends, Doris lived in mortal fear of a jealous, jilted lover from Cleveland. "If I'm found dead, he did it," she had reportedly told one of her friends. Others scoffed at this idea. "There's no guy in Cleveland. That's just a blind, see," one local gangster was quoted as saying (in a voice reminiscent of James Cagney, no doubt). "It's a stall to throw off suspicion. If the police are smart, they'll watch the fellow that gave them that bum steer. Someone in Harrisburg did Doris, and that's all there is to it."

On Thursday, October 1, police conducted a second search of the apartment but failed to find additional clues. "We've looked everywhere," said a frustrated Chief Shoemaker. "We've done everything but take up the carpet and look behind the wallpaper." No fingerprints were found inside the house. When asked if he would seek the cooperation of the State Police, Chief Shoemaker, perhaps aware of the State Police's poor track record of solving murder cases, said "definitely not." Meanwhile, Dauphin County authorities were trying to piece together details about Doris' life in Vermont, a period of time she had been loath to discuss.

THE EARLY LIFE OF DORIS WHITTMORE

Anna Doris Whittemore (which is her correct legal name) was one of eight children born to the Bentley family in Jericho, a tiny village twelve miles east of Burlington, Vermont, on August 28, 1901. Her parents, Mary Blood and Charles Bentley (brother of famed scientific photographer Wilson Alwyn Bentley), divorced while Doris was still a child.

While a young woman of sixteen, Doris married Robert Davis Whittemore of Burlington, but the marriage soon fell apart. By all accounts, Doris had enjoyed a normal, quiet life in Vermont. She had no prior criminal record in Vermont, and her reasons for choosing Harrisburg as a destination have never been determined.

The Jilted Lover

Despite the city's captain of detectives, Hyde Speese, being bedridden with an illness and unable to oversee the investigation, the progress made by the Harrisburg Police Department in such a short amount of time is nothing short of astonishing, especially considering the primitive methods used by law enforcement of the early 1930s. The secret of their success thus far had been the use of well-placed informants who loitered in city pool rooms, cafes, and restaurants. Within seventy-two hours of the murder, detectives had identified a dozen persons of interest and had questioned, detained, or interviewed nearly one hundred material witnesses. They had been successful in unearthing the details of the victim's doomed marriage and family history—secrets unknown to Doris' closest friends—and had even succeeded in tracking down the Cleveland man whom Doris had feared so deeply.

Shoemaker learned that Doris Whittmore had lived in Ohio with a man by the name of Peter Morei four years earlier, and Cleveland police managed to nab Morei within hours. Morei, who was once on the city's "black list" (the Cleveland version of a most wanted list), was able to prove that he hadn't been in Pennsylvania during the time of the murder and was released, though he was told by authorities not to leave town in case Chief Shoemaker wanted to question him personally at a later date.

One person whom authorities believed could shed some light on Doris' more recent affairs, however, was Lena Testa. Testa, who was an inmate at the Dauphin County Jail at the time, operated a brothel on Cherry Street, directly across the street from Doris' apartment. Doris had been one of Testa's call girls shortly after her arrival in Harrisburg. Much to the disappointment of city detectives, Testa refused to cooperate with the investigation. Police also checked with local banks in order to find out if Doris had made any suspicious deposits or withdrawals before her death. Only one financial institution—the Harrisburg Credit Exchange—had records pertaining to the victim, but these records were meager at best; Doris, like most folks engaged in questionable activities, preferred to pay for everything with cash. However, Chief Shoemaker noticed that some records listed the name "Doris Whittmoyer" instead of Whittmore (her preferred name) or Whittemore (her legal name). Presumably, these various spellings, though subtle, were intentional in order to throw off anyone who might be trying to track her down. Ironically, this flimsy and twisting paper trail might be one reason why her killer was never brought to justice.

Another issue hampering the investigation was the seal of silence. Underworld types and their cohorts, quite simply, did not "talk to coppers." The criminal underbelly of Harrisburg was an expansive tapestry with numerous interwoven threads: prostitutes profited from thugs, gamblers profited from bootleggers, dope pushers profited from prostitutes, thugs profited from dope pushers, and bootleggers profited from crooked cops and politicians. While scores of curious locals flocked to the Hauck Funeral Home to view the corpse of Doris Whittmore, most of her friends gave the place a wide berth since it was a good place to run into a detective. Yet these friends in low places, especially those employed in the sex trade, pooled their money to give Doris a decent burial in the event that no relative came forward to claim the body. One local gangster, according to the *Harrisburg Telegraph*, was overheard by an informant to remark: "Why don't her boyfriends get together and see that she has a decent burial? It's as little as they could do. She always played square with them."

RUMORS AND THEORIES

As with any sensational murder, rumors and theories about Doris' death created new angles for detectives to investigate. Some believed that the death was accidental in nature, perhaps the result of someone's carelessly thrown rock. In a state of panic, the unintentional killer may have dragged the body inside the house on Cherry Street. One clue that may support this theory is that Doris' body was placed in an upstairs bedroom, while her close friends stated that Doris always slept in a downstairs bedroom. Surely, a person intimately familiar with the victim would have known this detail.

A more popular theory was that Doris had been killed in a different location and the body taken to Cherry Street. The perpetrator, seeing that the house was guarded by officers with a warrant for Doris' arrest, lurked nearby in the shadows until the policemen departed at midnight. This would explain the missing murder weapon and the lack of fingerprints found inside the apartment. Chief Shoemaker didn't personally ascribe to this theory, but he promised that it was an angle he would investigate thoroughly. "We are leaving no stone unturned to find out who killed Doris Whittmore," promised Shoemaker.

On October 3, it was reported by the local press that an unidentified male had been seen exiting the front door of the Whittmore apartment in a hurry at eleven o'clock on the evening of the murder. William Franklin, the witness who claimed to have seen the mysterious visitor, made out a sworn statement to city detectives, furnishing a good description of the stranger. However, this contradicts the claim that two officers had staked out the house "for several hours" before leaving at midnight. Had the witness been mistaken about what time he had seen the man leave the apartment? Or were the two patrolmen derelict in their duties?

Alderman Hallman clarified the matter of the warrant, explaining that he had directed officers to arrest Doris on a morals charge and make a raid of the apartment, which Hallman believed was a den of prostitution. Upon further investigation, police learned that two anonymous callers had telephoned city hall earlier that afternoon asking if the Whittmore house had been raided. The second caller, who had telephoned thirty minutes after the first, spoke in the patois of an "underworld character." Based on this information, it seems likely that someone had been tipped off about the raid, which might explain how patrolmen failed to notice a man escaping from the house in a hurry right under their noses. Unfortunately, Chief Shoemaker was unable to comment on this development, as he had just left for Philadelphia to pursue a lead in the investigation, which, presumably, had something to do with Dominic "Clutch" DiPerna or Thomas Pinto, both of whom were Philadelphia natives.

Doris Whittmore's body being removed from her Cherry Street apartment by police-men. *Harrisburg Telegraph*, September 30, 1931.

Saved from Potter's Field

The body of Doris Whittmore remained at the morgue while authorities attempted to locate her next of kin. It was a race against the clock; if the body remained unclaimed for another twenty-four hours, it would be buried in an unmarked grave in potter's field. Fortunately, a brother-in-law from Connecticut, Lee Whittemore, had read about Doris' death in a local paper and boarded a train to Harrisburg to claim the body. Funeral services for Doris were held on the evening of October 6 at the Arthur Hauck funeral parlor on North Third Street in Harrisburg, with Reverend John Levan officiating. The funeral, by all accounts, was well attended, and Lee Whittemore had arrived just in time for the service. Doris lay in the open casket in her favorite dress, which her friends had picked out from her large and glamorous wardrobe. Standing at the head of the casket, Reverend Levan recited a passage from the Book of Isaiah known as "The Suffering Servant," which was a fitting choice for the occasion and served as a stirring tribute to the kind-hearted denizen of the night: He was despised and rejected by men, a man of sorrows, acquainted with grief. Like one from whom men hide their faces, he was despised and we esteemed him not. Surely he took on our infirmities and carried our sorrows; yet we considered him stricken by God, struck down and afflicted.

It was Lee Whittemore who revealed to the press a dark family secret and his sister-in-law's generous nature. "The last time I saw Doris was in November, three years ago," he said. "She had come to Meriden to pay the greater part of the costs of a funeral for a brother who had committed suicide in Newark, New Jersey. She went to Newark and arranged for his funeral there. If it had not been for her generosity her brother would have been buried in potter's field."

The following day, Doris' body was transported by train back to Vermont for burial in the Bentley family plot at Jericho Center Cemetery. It was truly a remarkable stroke of fate that her estranged brother-in-law happened to read a newspaper article about the Harrisburg woman's death; as a result, he managed to spare Doris' earthly remains from the same undignified fate from which she had rescued her own brother's body three years earlier.

While Lee Whittemore was in town, he was able to provide some interesting facts about Doris. She had always been generous with money, and she had helped her estranged family out of several financial predicaments, which seemed to be an ongoing issue with the Bentley clan. Until reading about her death in the paper, Whittemore had never suspected the true source of her income. According to Whittemore, Doris visited his home in Meriden on Christmas Day of 1927. She was accompanied by Peter Morei, whom she had introduced as her husband. "Last July we got a letter telling us that she had moved to Harrisburg following a quarrel with Morei in Cleveland," said Whittemore. "I have no idea who killed her. She never expressed fear of any one so far as I know."

The Prime Suspect

On October 7, Dominic "Clutch" DiPerna was released from police custody, while Harry Bittner of South Third Street was picked up for questioning as a possible witness. Meanwhile, Chief Shoemaker and Detective Yontz were in Cleveland questioning Peter Morei, who had previously been released after convincing Sergeant James Hogan that he wasn't in Pennsylvania at the time of the murder. Since alibis are only as good as the people who provide them, Shoemaker instructed Sergeant Hogan to detain Morei until witnesses from Harrisburg had a chance to see if they could pick him out of a line-up. It was no secret that Morei had been Shoemaker's prime suspect from the start of the investigation; when Doris told close friends that she was afraid of her husband, they assumed she had been referring to the man she left behind in Vermont, not the one she had left behind in Ohio.

William Franklin, the witness who claimed to have seen a man leaving the apartment, was taken to Cleveland, along with his wife. If Morei was the man that Franklin had seen on the night of Doris Whittmore's death, it was all but an open-and-shut case as far as Chief Shoemaker and Detective Yontz were concerned. Authorities in Cleveland were satisfied that Morei hadn't played a role in the Whittmore murder; because of his criminal reputation, police had been watching his movements long before Doris' death. During his initial questioning by Sergeant Hogan, Morei admitted that he had lived with Doris four years earlier but hadn't seen her in over a year. Morei denied leaving Ohio, and Cleveland detectives discovered that he had only left the city once in the previous two weeks, on a two-hour trip to a small city west of Cleveland.

When Morei was informed on October 8 that Harrisburg lawmen wanted to have a word with him, he voluntarily returned to police headquarters. After a series of questions had been asked by Detective Yontz, Chief Shoemaker was certain that Morei knew more about the murder than he claimed. The witnesses were then called into the room. Franklin carefully studied the suspect and said, "That's not the man." Franklin's wife, who had seen the mystery man loitering on the corner of Dewberry Street after leaving the Whittmore apartment, also failed to identify Morei. Chief Shoemaker and Detective Yontz looked at each other with shell-shocked expressions. They were so confident that Peter Morei had been the killer that they had brought along a warrant charging him with murder.

A Lull in the Investigation

Their investigation grounded like an airplane in bad weather, Shoemaker and Yontz returned to Harrisburg to lick their wounds and reassess their case. Several months passed without any new developments, and both the law-abiding citizens of the city and Ms. Whittmore's underworld friends were disappointed by the unfortunate turn of events. They recalled the 1929 case of candy store manager Verna Klink, whose killer was caught by Harrisburg police long before the victim's body had been found. The Klink case had essentially made celebrities of the city detectives, who were able to find clues which the State Police had overlooked (in fact, one of the city policemen who had worked the Klink case, Sergeant Patrick Hylan, became a contributor to *Real Detective Magazine*). For this reason, friends and relatives of Harrisburg crime victims had the utmost confidence in their hometown police department, while the State Police, they believed, was best left writing speeding tickets to motorists or directing traffic around highway crashes. That Chief Shoemaker and Detective Yontz would return from Cleveland empty-handed was unthinkable.

Until new leads developed, city police had to content themselves with making raids on the numerous "houses of ill repute" on Cherry

Street, with the hope of someone breaking the seal of silence. October 10 saw the raid of a house across the street from the Whittmore home, in which proprietress Gussie Cohen and an unidentified New Cumberland man with his pants down were nabbed. A raid of a Cherry Street pool room on October 29 resulted in the arrest and questioning of fourteen men, including proprietor Harry Crist, Peter Husic, Howard Shutter, and familiar faces Skeets Pinto and Clutch DiPerna. Slowly, but surely, detectives and their informants were gleaning information from the habitués of Harrisburg's red-light district, but it would take over a year to separate the wheat from the chaff.

A STAR (WITNESS) IS BORN

One of the more persistent thorns in the side of Harrisburg authorities was James Edward Maxwell, a thirty-year-old resident of Boas Street. Maxwell's crimes were usually of the minor variety, but his habitual disregard for the law kept patrolmen busy; in a span of just six months, he failed to show up for a court hearing over unpaid parking tickets, was stabbed during a knife fight with a neighborhood thug, and was arrested for burglarizing the home of Dr. J. L. Zimmerman. It was this last crime which led to his incarceration at the Dauphin County Jail. In early April of 1933, while awaiting trial in the burglary case, Maxwell made a stunning statement: On the night of Doris Whittmore's death, he had seen six men carrying a woman's body into a house on Cherry Street. Maxwell claimed the six men saw him and threatened to kill him if he told anybody about what he had witnessed. More importantly, Maxwell had not only seen the six men, but he also knew all of their names.

Within hours, four of the six men had been picked up by police. Michael Carricato was arrested on Chestnut Street by State Trooper Chester Engle and City Patrolman Thomas Knell. William Brashears was arrested on Market Street by City Detectives Harry Page and William Miller. Aldo Magnelli, who had been sent to prison three years earlier for assaulting federal prohibition agents, was arrested after he went to police headquarters in response to a telephone call by the assistant district attorney, Carl Shelley. The fourth man, James "Big Jim" O'Hara, was arrested in Pittsburgh and brought back to Harrisburg by Detectives

Page and Miller. After the four men had been taken to jail, they were brought before Alderman George Richards and formally charged with murder. The two other men seen by the witness, Harry Crist and Skeets Pinto, were still at large. Meanwhile, James Edward Maxwell was moved to a private cell for "safekeeping."

Chief of Police Shoemaker, who oversaw the capture of the four suspects, admitted to the press that these four suspects had not been arrested solely on Maxwell's statement. "There are other important details which we are unable to reveal at this time," said Shoemaker. He could not come up with an answer when asked why Maxwell had waited sixteen months to come forward about what he had seen, however. Interestingly, after the four suspects were in jail, police raided the Cherry Street home of Lena Testa, the twenty-eight-year-old prostitute who had given Doris her start in the world's oldest profession. Based on information they had gathered from their well-placed informants, police had reason to believe that Testa had been the one who drove Doris to Harrisburg after her breakup with Peter Morei. Testa's house was almost directly across the street from the Whittmore home. Chief Shoemaker, however, denied that the raid had anything to do with the Whittmore case.

Thomas Caldwell, a defense attorney known for representing Harrisburg underworld figures, was retained as legal counsel by the four men and promptly sought their release by bringing habeas corpus proceedings against Warden Hoy and Chief Shoemaker. On April 13, the habeas corpus hearings for Magnelli and O'Hara got underway, and at the outset of the hearing, the court sought to know why such proceedings were initiated after the defendants had already been held for court by Alderman Richards. Caldwell argued, quite correctly, that the alderman's actions were not legally binding: If the court found a lack of sufficient evidence to hold the defendants on murder charges, the alderman's decision could be overruled. Dr. Perkins, the physician who conducted the autopsy on Doris, was called to the stand by Assistant District Attorney Shelley and testified that the victim's death was caused by a hemorrhage resulting from a skull fracture. "That's it!" objected Caldwell. "There is not the least evidence that she was murdered!" On cross-examination, Dr. Perkins conceded that the fatal injury could have been caused by a car accident, a slip and fall, or by other accidental means.

The star witness for the Commonwealth, James Edward Maxwell, stated that he saw the six men drive up to the Whittmore home in an automobile owned by pool room proprietor Harry Crist at 2:30 in the morning, approximately seven hours before the maid found the body. Maxwell, who claimed that he was hiding in an alley about twenty feet away, saw three men get out of the car. According to Maxwell, it was Big Jim O'Hara who removed a bundle from the trunk. He could see only a pair of shoeless feet protruding from the bundle and a portion of a red evening gown. O'Hara carried the bundle into the basement of a different house on Cherry Street. Maxwell could not remember the exact address, but the house he was referring to could only have been the home of Lena Testa. After Maxwell had finished explaining how he had paused to watch the defendants, Caldwell asked, "Why didn't you go about your business?"

"I wish I had!" replied Maxwell.

Following the hearing, Magnelli and O'Hara were released on $5,000 bail. From a legal perspective, it was the proper decision; there was no evidence that Doris had been murdered, and even if she had been murdered, there was no proof that the murder occurred in Dauphin County. William Brashears and Michael Carricato were released on April 17. Interestingly, when Maxwell's burglary case finally went to trial on May 31, he was acquitted by a Dauphin County jury despite overwhelming direct evidence, thereby suggesting that being a star witness for the Commonwealth has its privileges.

THE CAPTURE OF CRIST

Much like James Edward Maxwell, Harry Crist had a long history of run-ins with law enforcement. As the operator of a pool room at the corner of Third and Cherry Streets, he had a close association with Harrisburg's shadiest characters, and his establishment was a frequent target of police raids, as this was the sort of place where one could go on any given evening to gamble, drink illegal liquor, and solicit a prostitute. In 1930, he was also one of four men arrested for brawling with federal prohibition agents during a raid of his pool hall. Crist, along with Aldo Magnelli, Richard Crist, and Anthony Comello, were sentenced to six months in jail for their actions.

Crist was taken into custody in Reading, Berks County, on April 17 by Detective Fred Marks. Marks and Berks County Assistant District Attorney Bertram Murphy transported Crist to police headquarters in Harrisburg, where a charge of murder was read to him. He was then deposited in the county jail. Crist's attorney, Maurice Yoffee, managed to have his client released on bail. Although Skeets Pinto was still on the loose, the murder trial for the five defendants was initially scheduled for the week of May 29. Assistant District Attorney E. Leroy Keen asked for a continuance, claiming that the prosecution needed more time to prepare its case. The trial was pushed back to September.

THE MURDER TRIAL THAT WASN'T

Pinto remained a fugitive as the grand jury convened on the afternoon of September 20, 1933. In addition, another key figure was nowhere to be found. The star witness, James Edward Maxwell, had disappeared without a trace. Since Maxwell's testimony would have been instrumental in securing an indictment, one can only imagine the sinking feeling in the stomachs of District Attorney Richards, Chief of Police Shoemaker, the city detectives, and everyone else who had worked so tirelessly to bring Doris Whittmore's killers to justice. Without Maxwell and Pinto, the grand jury had little choice but to ignore the murder charges. The five defendants walked out of the Dauphin County courthouse as free men. Despite this crushing setback, authorities vowed that the investigation would continue.

There is, however, some doubt as to whether the grand jury had enough evidence to return a murder indictment, even if Maxwell and Pinto had been present. During their investigation, detectives learned that Doris had attended a party at a cottage across the river in Summerdale, Cumberland County, on the final night of her life. Though nobody can prove that Doris was killed in Cumberland County, it would have been a miscarriage of justice for the defendants to be tried in a Dauphin County courtroom. But one thing remains clear—Doris was undoubtedly the victim of foul play. If her death had been accidental, there would have been no sensible reason for anyone to convey her bundled body back to Harrisburg in the dead of night or lay it out on a mattress in an upstairs bedroom for the maid to discover in the dull, gray light of a late September morning.

Unfortunately for friends and relatives of the victim, Cumberland County authorities had no interest in getting involved, and the case was never solved. In the decades following the Whittmore murder, the infamous red-light district of Harrisburg was bulldozed into oblivion, steamrolled in the name of progress. Today, high-rise apartment buildings cast long shadows over the spot where seedy brothels and smoky billiard halls once stood, and the shadowy men and women who frequented these establishments are long dead and buried.

THE LOWEST FORM OF HUMANITY

So, what became of the key figures in the Whittmore murder investigation? The disappearing witness, James Edward Maxwell, eventually came out of hiding, only to return to prison for receiving stolen property. In 1944, he was implicated in the murder of Harrisburg gambling parlor operator Lucius Baker. He was later acquitted. Aldo Magnelli made gambling his full-time profession and became a successful bookie and boxing promoter. In 1942, Peter Morei was sentenced to twelve years in prison by a Cleveland judge for operating a white slavery ring. "You are the lowest form of humanity," declared Judge Freed at Morei's sentencing. "I did not believe people could sink as low as you have. You are not entitled to any consideration whatever." Clutch DiPerna returned to Philadelphia, where he opened a market and supplemented his income as a bookie. Later in life, he would be stabbed inside his store during a robbery attempt but would go on to make a full recovery. The fates of Lena Testa, Skeets Pinto, Big Jim O'Hara, and Rosemund Dunlap are unknown, the details of the lives after the Whittmore murder lost in the dustbin of history. As for Doris' first maid, Almeda Morton, she became a frequent visitor to police headquarters. Her activities ran the gamut from making and selling moonshine to being on both the giving and receiving end of domestic battery resulting in bodily injury. Odds favor at least one of these individuals having dealt the deadly blow to the back of Doris Whittmore's skull. If not one of these individuals, then who else could it have been?

Perhaps there is a lesson, albeit a bitter one, to be learned in the tragic case of Doris Whittmore. Everybody appreciates a clean and tidy conclusion, but clean and tidy conclusions are more likely to occur in movies and television shows than in real life. In the real world, justice doesn't always prevail, and sometimes the bad guys win.

6

The Sugar Barrel Mystery

LUZERNE COUNTY

It has been written that no stretch of territory in the United States can show a darker record of mysterious deaths than the territory extending from Eckley to West Hazleton. Since the development of the "North Side" anthracite coal fields in the early 1860s, an untold number of men and women have died under mysterious circumstances or have been murdered by unknown killers. This portion of Luzerne County was home to immigrant miners from all parts of Europe, many of whom brought to America their ancient feuds and Old World vendettas. Ironically, they rekindled in the coal regions the very same prejudices which inspired them to leave their homes in Italy, Ireland, Wales, Poland, Ukraine, Lithuania, Hungary, Latvia, and other regions.

The infamous "Sugar Barrel Murder," which occurred on Ebervale Mountain in December of 1906, seems to fit the dark pattern that dates back to before the Civil War, when the region was suddenly deluged with impoverished immigrants whose loyalty was only to themselves and their immediate family. And, in the singular case of the Ebervale Mountain mystery, perhaps no such loyalty ever existed at all.

Early on the Sunday evening of December 17, 1906, Deputy Coroner Lamont received a telephone call informing him that a dead body had been found in a mountainside gully between the Ebervale and No. 3 Stockton collieries. Such a report was a regular occurrence for the deputy coroner; between mine accidents, drunken brawls, jealous husbands,

73

and dynamite mishaps, seldom did a day go by without such a telephone call. But little did Deputy Coroner Lamont realize at the time that he would soon come face to face with more than a dead body—he would soon be confronted with one of the most perplexing unsolved mysteries on the history of the North Side.

It was Patrick O'Donnell who made the gruesome discovery and placed the call to Dr. Lamont. O'Donnell was in the woods with his dogs when they began to show a strange uneasiness in the vicinity of a gully. This prompted O'Donnell to investigate, and he had gone off the path about thirty yards when he saw partially cremated human remains lying in the gully. He ran back to town as fast as his legs could carry him and notified Deputy Coroner Lamont.

The deputy coroner, accompanied by O'Donnell and several other concerned citizens, returned to the spot. Dr. Lamont made a closer examination. He discovered that the remains were those of a woman of indeterminate age, but even more shockingly, the body had been placed inside a wooden barrel before being set ablaze with the intention of obliterating all traces of the victim. It seemed that the killer had been fairly successful in this endeavor, as there was very little left of the body. In the waning minutes of daylight, the surrounding mountainside was hastily searched for clues before Lamont picked Michael Burns, Patrick Gallagher, and Daniel Gullick as part of a jury of inquiry. The men returned to Hazleton, where Lamont immediately went off in search of Poor Director Stauffer and Undertaker Philip J. Boyle, whose job it would be to gather up the remains and take them to the morgue.

"Perhaps we ought to wait until morning," said the undertaker. It was mid-December, and darkness had long since cloaked the mountain. Dr. Lamont would hear nothing of the sort; the body would be taken to the morgue come hell or high water, even if it took the men all night. Poor Director Stauffer wasn't home, so Undertaker Boyle hitched his horse to a wagon and drove to the lonesome spot where the remains had been found. The woman's charred body, and everything surrounding it, was loaded into the wagon. This included the wire binding rings and wooden staves of the burned barrel. This allowed police to determine that the barrel had been a sugar cask and the accelerant used was coal oil.

A CLOSER EXAMINATION

The remains were brought to the morgue around eleven o'clock that evening. The torso was badly charred, while both hands and the left foot were missing. The legs, arm, and head were twisted, showing that the woman had died before being stuffed into the barrel. The mouth was partially open, revealing a set of prominently protruding teeth. A slightly-worn high-heeled shoe, size five, was also among the ghastly relics that the undertaker had gathered up, along with the wire frame of a woman's hat.

It seemed unlikely that the burned body would yield any useful clues as to the identity of the killer, so police, led by County Detective Richard C. Jones, turned their attention to the remnants of the sugar barrel. As luck would have it, the top and bottom of the barrel had not completely burned, and on the bottom lid were stenciled letters: N & Co.—-noy City, Pa. This could only mean the barrel—and possibly the victim—had come from Mahanoy City, a hardscrabble coal-mining town in neighboring Schuylkill County, sixteen miles to the southwest. Records show one firm doing business in Mahanoy City at the time was Guinan & Co., which sold furniture, linoleum, and building supplies.

An autopsy was performed on Monday afternoon by Dr. Dyson, who determined that both legs had been broken below the knees. He also determined that the hands had been cut off before the body had been crammed into the barrel. This was an encouraging clue; there was little chance of fixing the location of where the murder had occurred if the hands had been burned away at the scene of the incineration, but if a woman's severed hand turned up in another place—such as Mahanoy City, for example—it would give detectives a place to focus their efforts. Several internal organs were examined by the physician but showed no signs of poison or internal injuries. The exact cause of death could not be determined.

One important clue was discovered by Dr. Dyson, however. A blackened chain with a small medal of the Virgin Mary was found around the woman's neck. This chain, along with a hat pin and large belt buckle, were turned over to Deputy Coroner Lamont.

GOSSIP AND THEORIES

Murders weren't uncommon in the tiny mining villages dotting the slopes of Ebervale Mountain, but the barrel mystery captured public interest like no other case in recent memory. There had been many cases throughout Luzerne County of bodies dismembered and packed into suitcases and barrels or tossed into rivers and mineshafts, but there was something truly abhorrent about hacking up a woman, stuffing her into a barrel, and burning it like household rubbish. This had to have been the work of a fiend, some argued, because most garden-variety killers simply would not have had the stomach for it. Others argued that more than one person had a hand in committing the gruesome deed, claiming that it would be quite difficult for a single individual to lug both body and barrel to the place of cremation in the mountain wilderness. Some insisted that the victim's throat must have been cut from ear to ear so as to allow the head to be twisted into the barrel with the rest of the body.

On Monday evening, a man from Stockton named Frank Slutak appeared at the morgue claiming that his twenty-year-old wife, Annie, had left their home two weeks earlier and never returned. He was fearful that his wife may have been the victim, but viewing the remains proved to be futile. The remains presented such a ghastly sight that Slutak wasn't sure what he was looking at, much less whom. He eventually concluded that the remains were not those of Annie, admitting that his wife had been a larger woman than the barrel victim.

Intense heat does cause bodies to shrink, however. While this grisly fact was certainly known in the early twentieth century, the exact extent of thermal shrinkage hasn't been determined until quite recently. In 2020, the *Journal of Forensic Sciences* published the results of a study by Sarah Ellingham and Michael Sandholzer, which involved incinerating sheep ribs at high temperatures and using X-ray microtomography to measure the structural changes of hard tissue. At 400 degrees Celsius (752 degrees Fahrenheit), a shrinkage of 14 percent was observed, while at 1,000 degrees Celsius (1,832 degrees Fahrenheit), a shrinkage of 45.5 percent was observed. Considering that, on average, the temperature of a campfire ranges between 1,500 and 1,650 degrees Fahrenheit, a wood fire aided by an accelerant (such as gasoline, kerosene, or coal oil) can burn even hotter. In other words, if Annie Slutak had stood sixty-five inches tall, she might've come out of the sugar barrel twenty inches shorter. Had modern forensic science been available to Detective Jones in 1906, it might've been possible to determine the actual height, weight, and age of the victim.

Two other names that popped up during the investigation was that of Mary Fedder, a "wayward" West Hazleton teenager who ran away from home some time before the discovery of the charred body, and May Anslovak, a young bride who disappeared after a fight with her husband. The names of other local girls with similar stories were gossiped around Luzerne County, as if the thought of the victim being a middle-aged woman had never crossed anyone's mind.

Constable Welsh Makes Arrest

The first arrest in the case came on the night of Monday, December 17, when Constable James Welsh arrested Sobiat Anslovak in the "Swamptown" section of Jeddo, about two miles east of Ebervale. Several months earlier, around Easter, Anslovak and May Manshinko mere married in the Polish Catholic church in Freeland. According to their Swamptown neighbors, the newlyweds fought constantly. After one particularly heated quarrel in November, May stormed out of the house and never returned. Friends and neighbors spent several weeks trying to track her down, but it was to no avail. It was if she had been swallowed up by the earth. Naturally, when news of the barrel murder reached Jeddo, most of the citizens jumped to the conclusion that the unfortunate victim was young Mrs. Anslovak. This included Constable Welsh, who paid a visit to the Anslovak home after hearing the rumors.

Constable Welsh reached the house at around nine o'clock and learned from the missing woman's cousin that Anslovak was working the night shift at the No. 4 mine in Jeddo. Welsh spoke at length with the cousin and reached the conclusion that there was enough probable cause to have Anslovak arrested. Fearing that Anslovak would flee from the vicinity upon learning about the discovery on the mountain, the constable went to the home of the mine foreman and explained the situation. The foreman accompanied Welsh down into the mine, where he placed Anslovak under arrest. He was transported to Freeland on the 11:45 trolley and taken to the office of Burgess George Hartman, where he was extensively questioned. Anslovak showed little concern during his grilling but broke down and wept after being placed into a cell.

According to the *Hazleton Sentinel*, the description Anslovak gave of his wife seemed to tally with that of the woman found on the mountain (but, to be fair, hundreds of women could've fit the description, so badly charred and mangled were the remains). May was described as being twenty years of age, 150 pounds, with light hair. In reality, none or all of these details may have matched the woman found in the burned sugar barrel. The detail that caught the attention of law enforcement was the coincidental shoe size—May Anslovak also wore size six shoes.

During his questioning, the twenty-eight-year-old miner denied that he and his wife quarreled frequently, claiming that they had only one major dust-up since their wedding day. However, he could provide no reason for her departure, other than stating that his wife often threatened to go back to Europe. According to the husband, May left home without taking any money with her and she had left in her bare feet, which, of course, would be exactly the sort of answer one might give if a trip to the gallows depended upon the identification of a woman's shoe. Adding to Welsh's suspicion was the fact that Anslovak was a powerful and muscular giant of a man who easily could have carried the barrel to the gully without assistance.

Authorities questioned every neighbor of Anslovak who was willing to speak. Some asserted that Sobiat had been acting strangely since May's disappearance; the rowdy, loutish miner seemed almost remorseful. It was also rumored that some children, while ice-skating near the Jeddo canal, had recently come across articles of woman's clothing and a bloodstained knife, which they did not touch. Though snow covered the ground, Constable Welsh immediately initiated a search for these objects. He found the articles of clothing—a red-checkered dress, a flannel petticoat, and a cotton chemise—but they turned out to be those of a young child. As for the knife, it turned out to be common table knife with a rusty blade. Welsh turned over these finds to Officer Thomas Morris of Hazleton.

Thousands View Remains

Ignatz and Veronica Nemcheck, relatives of the missing Swamptown woman, traveled to Hazleton on Tuesday to view the remains at Undertaker Boyle's funeral parlor. What little hair that remained on the skull was a darker shade, certainly not as light as May's hair, and the teeth were not the same. As the missing bride's sister, Veronica was certain that the remains were those of another woman entirely. The Nemchecks weren't the only visitors to the morgue that day; according to reports, nearly two thousand people visited Boyle's establishment to take a peek at the burned body and the grisly relics found on the mountain. No one was able to make a positive identification.

Detective Jones also made a careful examination of the remains that day and, based on the coloration of the hair and the Virgin Mary medallion, concluded that the woman was Italian.

Although the authorities could say with a high level of confidence that the woman in the barrel wasn't May Anslovak, her husband remained locked up in Freeland. He may not be the killer they had been seeking, but police felt that Anslovak knew more about his wife's disappearance than he had admitted to Burgess Hartman and Constable Welsh. The miner couldn't keep his story straight; he had told his captors at various times that his wife was across the sea in Europe, across the coal fields in the nearby borough of McAdoo, and in New York City. Anslovak said that he knew where in New York his runaway wife was living but couldn't recall the address. He insisted that a family in Ebervale knew the exact location, and Officer Mollick was dispatched to Ebervale to investigate. Anslovak was warned that he better not be sending the authorities on a wild goose chase or else he might be held in custody until his wife was found. This, of course, was an empty threat; due to lack of evidence, Anslovak was released two days later. Interestingly, the following year, in an unrelated case, Anslovak's house would be nearly destroyed by his enemies in a dynamite explosion. Newspaper clippings of the incident make no mention of Mrs. Anslovak, and it appears that she never returned.

THE BIANCO THEORY

A few miles away in Hazleton, it was whispered that the barrel victim was Mrs. Joseph Bianco, whose father, Rafael Marsicano, was murdered the previous June during a shootout with his son-in-law, Joseph Bianco. During the altercation, one of the shots had stuck Mrs. Bianco, seriously wounding her. She hadn't been seen since the murder trial, in which she gave testimony in favor of her husband, claiming that Joseph had shot her father in self-defense. Nevertheless, Joseph Bianco was convicted of murder and sentenced to Eastern Penitentiary in Philadelphia.

Mrs. Bianco made plenty of enemies after taking the stand to stick up for her father's killer and had received more than a few death threats for doing so. Four months before the discovery of the burned corpse, Mrs. Bianco sailed for Europe with her father-in-law and was scheduled to return to Hazleton in December. While some of her friends and relatives claimed that she had chosen to remain abroad (she had written a letter to her cousin intimating that she had no intention of returning to America), the popular opinion was that she was slain by a family member out of revenge upon her return. To many Italians, to side with a spouse instead of one's own birth parent, regardless of the circumstances, was an unforgivable sin. Adding credence to this theory is that Mrs. Bianco's hair color was the same as the hair on the barrel victim and that she also had protruding teeth.

Justice of the Peace Daniel T. McKelvey had a strong suspicion that the remains were those of Mrs. Bianco. On Wednesday, he went to the morgue but was unable to make a positive identification. Meanwhile, Coroner Dodson held an inquest in Hazleton. After the facts of the case had been presented by police officers from Hazleton, Freeland, and surrounding communities, the coroner's jury could only conclude that an unknown victim had been murdered by person or persons unknown.

DETECTIVE JONES AND THE BLACK HAND ANGLE

Despite the coroner jury's verdict, County Detective Jones would not accept defeat and vowed to solve the mystery, one way or another. "We cannot expect to gather all the details connected with a crime of this kind in a few days," stated Jones. "It requires hard and tedious work, and I, for one, will not admit that I have been defeated until I have run down every possible clue. I have found in my experience that some of the crimes which, at the first blush, appear to be unsolvable are cleared up by persistent work." Detective Jones urged the public to be patient; not even a week had passed since the finding of the body.

Detective Jones clung to his opinion that the murdered woman was an Italian and suggested that a detective of Italian ancestry ought to be brought in to assist in the investigation. "A man of Italian nationality, trained in the art of apprehending criminals, would be able to do excellent work in this county," declared Jones. He pointed to the case of the Cork Lane murder in the Italian section of Pittston a year earlier, which remained unsolved. The murder, in which the victim had been beheaded, took place near a mine shaft, and the head was later recovered from the bottom of the shaft. Jones believed the Cork Lane tragedy had been the work of the Black Hand—a catch-all term for Italian crime syndicates. But, because there were no Italians on the police force, it was impossible to infiltrate the ethnic gangs. "Because the county possessed no such available man, the gruesome murder, which shocked the entire community at the time, has been allowed to drop out of sight," stated Jones. With Christmas fast approaching, Jones feared the same outcome.

Tips from Afar
The sugar barrel mystery attracted attention across the country, and now law enforcement was tasked with wading through a slush pile of anonymous tips from faraway places. On December 20, Chief of Police Ferry received a bundle of newspaper clippings from South Bend, Indiana, from a man named C. W. Adams. Adams had read in one of the local papers a story about a teenager from Pittsburgh named Ruth Reed who disappeared under mysterious circumstances. When last seen, Reed was wearing a wire-brimmed hat and high-heeled shoes. Though Pittsburgh was 250 miles away from Hazleton and the odds of Ms. Reed being the barrel victim were fantastically slim, Chief Ferry contacted Pittsburgh police for additional information.

Chief Ferry also received a letter from Elkhart, Indiana, inquiring whether the victim had false teeth. The sender's niece, who had false teeth, had been missing from her home in Connecticut since October. Ferry kindly wrote back that the teeth in the victim's skull were all natural. Detective Jones received a letter from a Lima, Ohio, barber who was looking for a lost sister with false teeth. Though authorities carefully read every out-of-state letter, they found themselves no closer to solving the mystery than when they had opened their investigation.

A CHRISTMAS EVE BURIAL

Initially, the authorities planned to have the remains of the barrel victim buried on December 21 at the almshouse potter's field in Laurytown. However, contributions from generous citizens, perhaps heartened by the spirit of the holiday season, allowed Undertaker Boyle to purchase a plot in the Vine Street Cemetery. On December 24, the remains were quietly conveyed to the graveyard with neither fanfare nor ceremony and Undertaker Boyle buried somebody's missing daughter in the cold ground beneath a simple wooden marker upon which the word "Unknown" had been painted. His placing under the sod yesterday the charred body of the murdered girl moves from sight, and possibly from our minds, a murder mystery that has had no equal in the coal regions for its atrocity, reported the *Hazleton Sentinel*. The burial made it impossible to examine the remains unless a judge issued an order of exhumation. This effectively put the nail in the coffin of the investigation, unless someone were to come forward with new and convincing information or to confess to the crime.

The last promising tip of the year came on December 28, 1906, when a woman from Wilkes-Barre telephoned police headquarters and stated her belief that the murdered woman was her sister. County Detective Jones and City Detective Jeff Ruddy went to the home of the woman, whose name was never revealed but returned to Hazleton with less faith in cracking the case than before they departed. By year's end, Detective Jones had become ambivalent about the sugar barrel mystery; he held fast to his belief that the case had all the markings of an Italian Black Hand slaying but had no way of proving it.

ADDITIONAL CLUES DISCOVERED

In the years following the chilling discovery made on Ebervale Mountain by Patrick O'Donnell, the occasional rumor would breathe some life back into the forgotten mystery and the occasional out-of-town tip would be checked out by detectives. In January 1907, Inspector William McLaughlin of the New York City Detective Bureau was following the trail of Catherine Arozone, a missing teenager, when he recalled the Hazleton barrel mystery and contacted Chief Ferry for additional information. Dental records provided by the New York detective did not match those of the barrel victim. Around the same time, two detectives from the borough of Luzerne apprehended an Italian man in Allentown on suspicion of knowing something about the murder, but this proved to be yet another dead end.

When a spell of warm weather came along in early January, Ebervale Mountain was free of snow for the first time in several weeks and dozens of amateur sleuths took to the woods in search of overlooked evidence. Excitement ran high on January 6 when two young men, Bernard McGovern and William Cannon, returned from the murder scene with a number of fire-blackened articles worn by the victim. These included a hat pin, two garter buckles, two hair combs, part of a fur neck stole, and two rings. One ring was of a braided, gold-plated wire, while the other ring was missing three gemstones. There appeared to be an initial on one of the rings, but the combination of fire, water, and other elements had made the engraving unreadable. The men had also found bloodstained straw, which had evidently been used to assist in burning the body.

McGovern and Cannon turned over their finds to Justice of the Peace Daniel McKelvey, who determined that the victim had been dressed up at the time of her death and that, in all likelihood, the murder had occurred during the evening. These newly discovered clues, however, did not lead to an identification, and police issued a statement to the press declaring that the bottom had dropped out of the barrel murder investigation.

Detective Jones may not have discovered the identity of the killer, but he wasn't shy about pinning the blame on those who impeded his efforts. He fixed a great deal of blame on the Luzerne County commissioners for not offering a reward for information leading to the arrest of the guilty party. The commissioners defended their decision by arguing that it was never proven that the murder had actually been committed within the county limits; for all they knew, the body could have been transported to Ebervale Mountain from anywhere, and why should they pay out a sum of money for the capture of a killer from a different part of the state? The detective's accusation did not sit well with county officials, of course. Jones continued to butt heads with county officials, leading to his demotion to assistant county detective by District Attorney Abram Salsburg. When Salsburg finally demanded Jones' resignation in 1909, the pugnacious detective refused. When a reporter asked Jones, whose career was effectively over, when he planned on relinquishing his post, Jones replied, "When I'm good and ready." Nonetheless, he was unceremoniously booted from the assistant detective's office a few days later when District Attorney Salsburg appointed Charles Norris to the position of assistant county detective.

THE GERMAN VISITOR AND THE MARVELOUS FAYS

Just when the citizens of Luzerne County had forgotten about the crime, the barrel mystery was thrust into the spotlight after a strange visit to Undertaker Boyle's funeral parlor on South Wyoming Street by two men in January of 1908. The men, who were of German ancestry and had come from West Hazleton, asked Boyle if he had any photographs of the charred corpse. One of the men, who refused to give his name, explained that he had a daughter who had run away from home and hadn't been heard from in years. Boyle shook his head but directed the visitors to one of the local photography studios, as the proprietor had taken a picture of the remains for a magazine. Boyle hadn't taken the visitor's claims too seriously—until he mentioned that his daughter owned several rings and had a fondness for fashionable clothing. The undertaker also learned that the man's daughter had run away from home because she was afraid of a certain man who was extremely jealous of her. The details of the man's story certainly matched the description of the barrel victim, but the entire episode seemed too strange to be believable. Why would a father wait so long to come forward?

The investigation was reopened, and it was reported that the German visitor to the morgue was a man named Henry Malcolm, who was not a resident of the Hazleton area at the time of his daughter's disappearance or when the crime was discovered. In fact, he hadn't learned about the barrel murder until after he settled in West Hazleton. Unfortunately, police were unable to reach a definite conclusion; Ms. Malcolm might have been the victim, but with the body long buried and the victim's belongings eroded by time and the elements, it was impossible to tell for certain.

One person who did claim to know for certain the identity of the victim was Mrs. Fay, one half of a famous husband-and-wife vaudeville team specializing in mind-reading and psychic predictions. The Marvelous Fays, as they were billed, enthralled opera house audiences throughout the United States with their "Ask the Fays" act, in which Anna Eva Fay revealed the age and provenance of family heirlooms, the whereabouts of missing valuables, and the itineraries of audience members' upcoming vacations, among other things. Handbills promoted Anna Eva as a "daughter of India, possessing the art of the East India Yogi and the famed Mahatmas" (though she was really from a small town in Ohio), and the act was so well-known in its time that even iconic vaudeville historian Joe Laurie Jr. devoted a paragraph to the Fays in his acclaimed 1953 book *Vaudeville: From the Honky-Tonks to the Palace*.

When the Fays played a weeklong engagement at the Grand Opera House in Hazleton in early February 1908, it was just a matter of time before someone brought up the sugar barrel murder during the "Ask the Fays" portion of the act. While deep in her trademark trance, Anna Eva announced that the victim was a foreign girl named "Mary Pohatah" from Mahanoy City who did not speak English. The audience clamored for more details, but Mrs. Fay snapped out of her trance without answering any more questions. Local papers were astonished and proclaimed Mrs. Fay the genuine psychic article. After all, how could a famous performer who hobnobbed with the likes of New York theater impresario Willie Hammerstein (who, incidentally, served as the Fay's publicist at the time) possibly know about a Podunk coal town like Mahanoy City?

Anna Eva Fay. *The Kentucky Post*, May 13, 1927.

The answer to this question is that Mrs. Fay, like any good professional stage psychic, did her homework and possessed a remarkable talent for memorization. Scranton, Wilkes-Barre, Hazleton, and other cities in the coal region were regular stops on the vaudeville circuit, and Hammerstein was a heavy hitter with a large and well-paid staff who had little difficulty researching big news stories from the cities on the Fays' tour. When the charred body was found in December of 1906, virtually every newspaper in the region noted that Mahanoy City was stamped onto the bottom of the sugar barrel. And had folks from Luzerne County been reading papers like the *New York Times*, they would've known that Mrs. Fay was embroiled in an ongoing legal dispute with her magician son, John Tudman Fay, and several former employees who produced a rival stage show exposing Anna Eva's fraudulent methods (the case even reached the New York Supreme Court). During the legal battle, Mrs. Fay's former employees testified that they would dig up information about audience members in the cities in which the Marvelous Fays performed.

As an interesting sidenote, John Tudman Fay's rival show was a big draw at the time of the barrel murder but soon fizzled out. The show began to lose money, and in December of 1908, John T. Fay committed suicide by shooting himself in the head in his Oakland, California, hotel room. When writing about the financial struggles of this rival act, vaudeville historian Joe Laurie Jr. remarked: It seemed that audiences didn't like to be disillusioned—they would rather be fooled.

THE END OF THE TRAIL

By 1911, the case of the sugar barrel mystery was cold but not quite frozen. The year started with a tantalizing theory involving a missing daughter from an affluent West Hazleton family. Dicky Powell of Edwardsville was the county detective at the time, and Powell believed the murder victim to be a girl named Annie Garlow, a noted belle who had fallen in love with an Italian "Black Hand" member and left home to live with him. As the live-in lover of a mobster, Annie was privy to all sorts of damning information about underworld deeds, and it was claimed by police that Annie had intimate knowledge about the murder of a junk dealer named Joseph Moran, whose body had been wrapped in an oil-soaked blanket and burned on a mining road just north of Jeddo eleven years earlier. Annie, it was said, had been "bumped off" because she knew too much. Newspapers across Pennsylvania bragged in bold print that the famous barrel mystery had finally been solved. However, there was only one way to put the matter to rest for good; Annie was known to have a gold filling in an upper tooth, and Detective Powell promptly called for the exhumation of the body buried four years earlier in the Vine Street Cemetery. As there exists no record of this exhumation, it is doubtful that it ever took place. Surely, somebody familiar with the case (or any of the thousands of people who viewed the remains at the morgue) would have noticed the presence of a gold tooth. Whatever became of Annie Garlow is unclear.

The case cooled until summer, when a letter from a small town in Austria was delivered to Hazleton inquiring about Mary Klater, a domestic servant who had worked in McAdoo and Hazleton before disappearing under mysterious circumstances. Several years earlier, Ms. Klater had written a letter to her parents in Austria in which she stated that she had saved up enough money to return home and live a life of ease and comfort. That was the last time anyone heard from her. An investigation revealed that Ms. Klater left for New York after withdrawing several hundred dollars from a Hazleton bank, but the investigation also revealed that she embarked on this journey after the barrel murder had already taken place. The letter from Austria failed to produce a solution to one mystery, but it did create another; to this day, no one knows why Mary Klater failed to reach her destination.

While it is unlikely the mystery of the charred corpse of Ebervale Mountain will ever be solved, it is likely that Detective Jones had been on the right track all along. Jones undoubtedly recalled the famous case in 1903 in which a man named Madonia Benedetto was killed and stuffed into a sugar barrel in New York. In the years following the Ebervale Mountain murder, several similar killings occurred throughout the country. The mutilated body of ex-convict Francesco Manzella was discovered in a barrel in Rochester in 1911, while Guiseppe Pasquale was found inside a barrel in Utica in 1915. Gaspara Candella's body, which had been stabbed sixty-two times, was found stuffed into a barrel in Brooklyn in 1918. In virtually all the cases that were solved and prosecuted, the murders had been committed by Italians involved in organized crime, and this motive behind these murders was almost always revenge for snitching and squealing.

7

The Bread Man's Last Delivery

NORTHUMBERLAND COUNTY

Of Pennsylvania's sixty-seven counties, perhaps none has a greater number of unsolved murders per capita than Northumberland. After the murder of a miner named Michael Wanzie occurred in the village of Natalie in June of 1905, one local paper pointed out that his was the 107th murder in county history and that only one person up to that date had been arrested, tried, and convicted of the crime of first-degree murder (not surprisingly, Wanzie's killer, Frank Riko, was eventually acquitted of the crime). While the identities of many of these cold-blooded killers were known to authorities and the public at large, a greater number of killers have never been identified, earning Northumberland County a reputation as a "murderer's paradise."

The rise of organized crime during and after the Prohibition Era, coupled with political corruption and ineffectual law enforcement, only worsened Northumberland County's murder problem. One unsolved murder of the Prohibition Era was that of Edward "Claude" Haas, whose strangled body was discovered in the coal mining town of Trevorton a year after his disappearance.

Three days after fifty-three-year-old Claude Haas disappeared on April 30, 1932, State Police at the Tharptown barracks still believed that he was alive, even though Claude's own father thought otherwise. Samuel Haas was certain that his son's body would be found somewhere in the mine-scarred mountains, in the vicinity of the North Franklin Colliery.

It was in this vicinity, just south of Trevorton, where police had already found Claude's empty wallet and other personal belongings. The reason police believed that Claude was still alive was because no body had been found, nor a drop of blood, despite numerous spent cartridges scattered on the ground near the spot where Claude's personal effects were discovered. The reason Samuel Haas believed that his son was dead was because Claude's final customer had been Donald Bastress, and everyone knew that Bastress was a bad, bad man.

Claude Haas, of 816 North Sixth Street, Shamokin, worked as a delivery man for the Shamokin Baking Company. Standing at five feet, eight inches and weighing 265 pounds, the middle-aged widower appeared to his customers as a jovial, good-natured fellow who certainly had eaten his fair share of baked goods, and his pleasant disposition brought almost as much joy to his customers as the contents of his delivery truck. On the morning of Saturday, April 30, a boy named Harry Strine found a note tacked to a tree in the yard of George Bastress in Trevorton. The note was intended for Claude, and it instructed him to "bring eleven loaves of bread and four dozen cup cakes" and "to come alone." Strine, as he had done many times before, delivered the note to Claude. The reason for this level of secrecy was because Bastress' adopted son was hiding from the law; he was the prime suspect in a string of robberies across the Coal Region and was wanted for passing bogus checks. The wording of this note indicated that Bastress had been ordering baked goods from Claude for quite some time and that a rendezvous point had long since been chosen.

When Claude failed to return his delivery truck to the Shamokin Baking Company at five o'clock, his employer grew concerned and notified the authorities. Claude was neither irresponsible nor untrustworthy, so the employer's first thought was that an accident had occurred. Shamokin city police found the delivery truck parked on West Arch Street, but there was no sign of the driver. The loaves of bread and cupcakes were still inside the vehicle, though the key was missing from the ignition. A check with the bakery showed that Claude had left Shamokin with eleven loaves of bread early that morning, which he had intended to deliver to Trevorton. It was a six-mile trip that should've taken no longer than thirty minutes.

The following morning, Claude's son, Samuel, organized a search party and combed the woods near Trevorton, where he believed his father was last seen. Accompanied by his brothers-in-law, Don Herb and Art Evans, the three men scoured the hills and culm banks from sunrise to sunset but found no trace of Claude Haas. Meanwhile, Corporal Earl Pepple and troopers Cyril Edwards and John Scheidel of the State Police, assisted by County Detective Donald Zimmerman, were running down leads. They learned that Claude's final delivery had been to John Bastress, and that Donald Bastress was known to hide out in a shack in the woods just south of Trevorton. They, too, went into the woods in search of clues, but only found Sam Haas, Herb, and Evans.

Things got complicated after word of Claude's disappearance spread around Shamokin. Several witnesses came forward claiming they had seen Claude get out of the delivery truck at around seven o'clock in the evening and walk down Arch Street, but these descriptions varied wildly; some witnesses claimed to have seen a portly fellow, others a thin fellow. One witness, who claimed to know Claude personally, said he saw the missing delivery man eating alone in a Shamokin restaurant around midnight. Troopers Edwards and Scheidel canvassed the city on foot, stopping every place Claude might've stopped. After they interviewed Strine, authorities refocused their search on Trevorton. After going door to door, they learned that a bakery truck had been seen parked along the unpaved road leading to the North Franklin Colliery dam. Upon visiting the dam, the troopers found papers and order forms from the Shamokin Baking Company and realized that, if a body was to be found, it was likely to be found at the bottom of the reservoir.

THE DRAINING OF THE RESERVOIR

With permission from officials of the Philadelphia and Reading Coal and Iron Company, the dam was dynamited by colliery employees John Blanksby, Thomas Arrison, and Elias Ebersole as the State Police looked on. The Trevorton Fire Company assisted in pumping out the remaining water. Attired in a bathing suit, Robert Nye waded through the enormous shallow puddle but found no sign of a body. They did find Claude's wallet, however, containing the missing man's driver's license and a gasoline receipt but no money. It appeared that robbery was a likely motive, and their attention turned to Donald Bastress. State Police then questioned Mr. Bastress, who said that he had seen no sign of his fugitive son for about two months. This unlikely story seemed to appease authorities.

On Wednesday, May 4, Claude's son, Samuel, made a futile search of nearby Irish Valley, after he had been informed that a man resembling Bastress had been seen in the vicinity driving a Hudson sedan. Frank Dennen, a family friend, joined Samuel in his sweep of Irish Valley, though State Police refused to get involved. The May 5, 1932, edition of the *Shamokin News-Dispatch* reported that authorities had come to the conclusion that Claude had disappeared of "his own accord" after throwing his wallet into the North Franklin Colliery reservoir and that there was nothing more they could do. To Claude's relatives, it was as if the State Police had said, "We already dynamited the dam and questioned John Bastress, what more do you expect from us?"

This lackadaisical approach did not sit well with Ida Haas, sister of the missing delivery man. Miss Haas insisted that Claude had never been absent from home for any length of time and that he had always made it a point to notify relatives of his whereabouts. Meanwhile, as Samuel Haas busied himself doing the job the State Police refused to do, the office of the Midvalley Colliery was robbed. Less than three months earlier, Bastress had been accused of a robbery at the Natalie slope of the Colonial Colliery and had also been accused of selling iron and steel pilfered from other local collieries to a Danville junk dealer. Even though Bastress had a warrant out for his arrest, and even though the Midvale robbery fit Bastress' modus operandi, Corporal Earl Pepple of the Tharptown detail of the State Police had refused to take action, claiming that the robbery was out of his jurisdiction. The *News-Dispatch* reported the following: Corporal Pepple referred the information to the Wyoming detachment of the state police without obtaining details of the robbery. This caused many people to scratch their heads; Tharptown was less than a mile from Shamokin and only seven miles from Trevorton, while the Wyoming barracks was located over seventy miles away.

THE HUNT FOR DONALD BASTRESS

County Detective Zimmerman had reliable information indicating that twenty-four-year-old Donald Bastress was hiding out in Reading, Berks County, but was powerless to go after him. Despite a lengthy rap sheet, Bastress had been paroled shortly before Claude's disappearance, even though the brash fugitive had confessed to tearing up colliery railroads and coal washery buildings and selling the iron as scrap. However, as the number of robberies continued to pile up in the two-week period following Claude's disappearance, Zimmerman vowed to bring Bastress to justice. All he had to do was wait until Bastress was spotted in Northumberland County. He didn't have to wait very long.

On May 16, three men from the Reading area—Harry Kramer, Stanley Parellas, and Frank Williams—arrived in Shamokin to meet a man they knew only as J. J. Tyler, who had rented their trucks to haul cattle and scrap metal from Shamokin to Reading. The men had come to collect their payment, only to discover they had been fleeced. They reported this matter to the police, stating they had answered an advertisement in a Reading paper. The ad had been placed by J. J. Tyler, whom Detective Zimmerman strongly suspected was an alias used by Bastress. Further investigation proved that Zimmerman was correct; the men from Reading said they had met with "J. J. Tyler" in Trevorton ten days earlier, and their description matched that of the fugitive.

According to Kramer, Parellas, and Williams, the three men had unwittingly assisted Bastress in hauling stolen cows from Irish Valley to Reading. Bastress, driving a flashy Hudson sedan, had represented himself as the son of a wealthy Sunbury cattle trader and claimed that the cows had been purchased legally from Irish Valley farmers. Not surprisingly, the report of the Bastress sighting in Irish Valley that the State Police ignored (but was taken seriously by Samuel Haas and Frank Dennen) had proved to be correct.

While Corporal Pepple had yet again missed an opportunity to catch the fugitive, Detective Zimmerman and Trooper Cyril Edwards traveled to Reading, intent on taking Bastress into custody. Thanks to the information given to them, it was learned that the men from Reading had also been duped into transporting fourteen tons of stolen metal

Donald Bastress. *Shamokin News-Dispatch*, April 21, 1941.

from the Luke Fidler Colliery in Shamokin and eight tons of metal from the North Franklin Colliery in Trevorton. Bastress had duped the men by insisting that the deliveries be carried out at night so as to avoid interfering with the daily operations of the coal companies. Bastress had promised to pay the men on May 16, and after "J. J. Tyler" failed to make an appearance, they had gone to the city police. Interestingly, Shamokin Chief of Police Charles Levan had received an anonymous tip a week earlier that Bastress had recently been seen in town, wearing a green sweater that matched the color of the sweater Claude had been wearing on the day of his disappearance. Levan and his officers scoured Shamokin for days but were unable to find him.

In the early hours of Thursday, May 19, Zimmerman and Edwards visited the Reading detail of the State Police, and they nabbed Bastress in a neighborhood pool hall. Bastress was held overnight in the city jail and transported back to Northumberland County the next morning. Reading junk man Samuel Robertson was also arrested after Zimmerman and Edwards identified twelve tons of brass, copper, iron, and other materials that had been stolen from Northumberland County collieries. The three men whose complaint had led to Bastress' arrest were also detained as material witnesses, in the belief that they might have information that could solve the mystery of Claude Haas' disappearance.

BASTRESS BREAKS HIS SILENCE

Donald Bastress admitted his role in being the ringleader of a loosely organized gang of robbers and bandits, though he insisted that he had nothing to do with the disappearance of Claude Haas. His lengthy rap sheet seemed to confirm this; Bastress had never been known to use violence, or even weapons for that matter, in any of his criminal activities. During his interrogation by police, Bastress admitted that he knew Claude and liked him, but he had been so busy with his own criminal activities that he hadn't even heard about the bread man's disappearance.

But what happened to Claude that caused his personal belongings to be found near the North Franklin Colliery? And how did his delivery truck come to be abandoned on the streets of Shamokin?

To find the answer to these questions, State Police enlisted the aid of the Kane Detective Agency, which had an office inside the Newberry Building on Independence Street in Shamokin. In the presence of Detective Bert Kane and several members of the local and State Police, Bastress signed a lengthy confession claiming responsibility for dozens of robberies, from the Luke Fidler breaker to the Snydertown Knitting Mills, and from scores of farms in Irish Valley and Augustaville. He had even stolen a length of telephone wire and telephone poles at Hunter Station from the Pennsylvania Power & Light Company by posing as a utility worker. Yet he steadfastly denied knowing anything about Claude's disappearance. He admitted that Claude had delivered food to him on several previous occasions but had always considered him a friend. According to Bastress, he had found the Shamokin Baking Company delivery truck abandoned near the colliery and drove it back to Shamokin because he thought Claude had been detained by some sort of emergency and didn't want him to get into trouble with his employer.

After the confession had been signed, authorities continued to hold steady to their belief that Claude had vanished of his own volition, and some intimated that he might've fled because Claude, like the three men from Reading, had been duped into committing illegal acts. Others suspected that the mild-mannered delivery man, who had not been romantically involved with anyone since the death of his wife, had run off with a young woman who had stolen his heart.

On June 1, Bastress was one of five inmates who escaped from the Northumberland County Prison in Sunbury, where he was being held while awaiting trial. This jailbreak is noteworthy because his fellow escape artists included Calvin Tyson and Charles O'Neill, two young bandits who would later achieve notoriety for killing a prison guard in Pikesville, Maryland. Unfortunately for Bastress, his twenty-five-foot leap from the jail wall to the sidewalk on River Avenue resulted in several broken bones and he was promptly recaptured. He would later serve his ten-to-twenty-year sentence for robbery at the Eastern Penitentiary in Philadelphia.

The Finding of the Body

While State Police had given up on solving the mystery of Claude Haas' disappearance, Samuel Haas refused to stop searching for his father. In September, upon learning that the body of an unidentified man was found in Millerstown, Samuel and his father's former housekeeper, Sadie Rohrbach, traveled to Perry County to view the corpse. The only similarity was that the unknown man had been wearing a green sweater at the time of his death. They returned to Shamokin undaunted and vowed to keep searching.

It was three teenagers from Trevorton who found Claude's body on the afternoon of July 17, 1933, while picking apples in the woods near the North Franklin Colliery. Stanley Pennypacker, Roy Long, and Donald Wolf had stopped to rest at the foundation of the colliery mule barn, which had been razed a month earlier, when one of the boys began probing the sawdust with a stick. Pennypacker noticed a scrap of clothing sticking out of the sawdust, and when he pulled up the material, the arm of a dead man was exposed. The teenagers ran to the colliery office and notified Charles Morlock, a security officer for the Reading Coal and Iron Company. Morlock called the State Police in Tharptown, and Sergeant Reese L. Davis and Private William Keuch rushed to the scene. They were soon joined by County Detective Zimmerman and Coroner A. J. Ancerawicz.

The body of Claude Haas was found with a burlap sack over the head, and a length of insulated copper wire was twisted tightly around the neck. A hole in the back of the skull indicated that Claude had been struck with a heavy object, and evidence seemed to suggest that after being knocked unconscious, Claude had been strangled with the wire before being hastily buried inside the stable. Samuel Haas was called to identify the body, but the remains were so badly decomposed that he couldn't be certain that it was his father.

It was the housekeeper, Sadie Rohrbach, who made the identification at the Campton Funeral Parlor through the victim's dental bridgework, though she was not permitted to view the remains because of the advanced state of decomposition. Rohrbach told the detective that Claude had injured his left foot shortly before his disappearance and had been wearing a bandage. The bandage was found at the scene. The housekeeper also recognized the dead man's shoes. "I'll never forget the night before he disappeared," she said. "We sat in the kitchen and put new rubber soles on his shoes." As the remains were little more than a skeleton, they were immediately buried at the Shamokin Cemetery.

WAS ROBBERY THE MOTIVE?

After the decaying remains of Claude Haas had been pulled from the sawdust, Coroner Ancerawicz and Detective Zimmerman made a thorough inspection of the body. Claude had been dressed in the same green sweater and gray trousers he wore on the morning he left home. The pockets of his trousers were turned inside out, which seemed to indicate robbery, or that the killer had been searching for something. Naturally, suspicion once again fell on Donald Bastress. Bastress, after all, had been charged with stealing copper wire, among other things, from local collieries, and copper wire had been used to strangle Claude. Bastress was also known to have used a shack in the woods near the colliery as a hideout, and Bastress (going by the name of J. J. Tyler) had been operating in the vicinity as the son of a wealthy cattle trader on the day of Claude's death. Yet Bastress had already built up a lucrative criminal enterprise and had done so without violence; why should he risk it all for the paltry contents of a bakery delivery man's wallet? Did Claude Haas unexpectedly encounter Bastress in the middle of an illegal transaction? And did Bastress murder the portly delivery man to silence him?

The possibility exists that Claude may have run into one of Bastress' associates during his fateful trip to Trevorton and that Claude had seen this man clearly enough to make a positive identification. Bastress may have seen Claude as a friend, but the associate might have seen Claude as a risk or as an unfortunate stranger who happened to be in the wrong place at the wrong time. In light of Bastress' aversion to physical violence, this seems like a more plausible explanation. However, there was one incident in 1928 that might have some bearing on the case.

In the late 1920s, Claude purchased the Belmont Restaurant, which was located next to the Dime Bank Building. Claude, who was also the former owner of the Eagle Hotel Lunch, changed the name of the

Belmont to the American in July of 1928. Shortly after opening the American, he foiled a burglary attempt. Claude was closing up for the night when he chased away a suspicious-looking person from the front of the building. Then, while making an investigation, he discovered another would-be burglar climbing a ladder in the rear of the building. Both men made a getaway and were never identified. Is it possible that Claude's killer was one of the men he had chased away four years earlier? It's certainly a stretch, but it's an angle that police never investigated.

THE CASE GOES COLD

A new angle in the case developed at the end of July when the sister of one of Donald Bastress' associates told authorities that he had made a peculiar statement to her brother while both men were being treated in the prisoner's ward of the Mary Packer Hospital in Sunbury. Bastress, who was being treated at the time for injuries sustained in his jailbreak attempt, had reportedly told his friend, "I know where Haas is, and they'll never find him." Although police gave very little credence to this "tip," the investigation into Claude's murder continued but came to a close in April of 1934 after a month-long investigation by two undercover State Police officers failed to turn up additional evidence. "Two special operatives of the State Police spent an entire month in the region, closely investigating every lead in the case, but without learning anything which would warrant an arrest," said District Attorney Robert M. Fortney. "The case is as much a mystery today as it was when Haas first disappeared."

Despite a mountain of circumstantial evidence—Bastress had the means and the opportunity to kill Claude—no one was ever charged for the crime. Bastress admitted to driving the delivery truck from Trevorton to Shamokin but had no alibi. Yet, the Tharptown detail of the Pennsylvania State Police were powerless to do anything about it. They had in their possession the murder weapon, but a length of insulated copper wire isn't the same thing as a smoking gun.

"THE SEVEN VETERANS"

Donald Bastress was paroled in 1938 and was granted early release through the efforts of Philadelphia social workers. During his incarceration,

Bastress devoted himself to religious study and volunteer work inside the prison. However, it didn't take him long to return to his old ways. In April of 1941, Bastress and Harry Kessler of Northumberland were arrested by Philadelphia police and held as suspects in a series of robberies. Bastress and Kessler had obtained employment with the Budd Manufacturing Company of Philadelphia, and it was there the men formed partnerships with several notorious bandits. Known as "The Seven Veterans" because all members of the group were career criminals, this gang participated in a wave of hold-ups of mine workers in Pottsville, Minersville, and Tamaqua.

Over time, the exploits of the "Seven Veterans" showed signs of becoming increasingly violent. During this crime spree, the Acme Market in Sunbury was robbed at gunpoint, allowing the bandits to make off with $900. Bastress, along with Philadelphia outlaws Joseph Matthews and John Andrews, also held up a Sunbury liquor store that same week, robbing clerk William Snyder of $355. In total, there were over thirty hold-ups in the region during a two-week period in April, and police were certain that Bastress' gang was behind all of them. However, when asked about the unsolved murder of Claude Haas, State Police Corporal Hochreiter said that it was "now too late" to question Bastress about the killing. A curious statement, considering there is no statute of limitations on murder.

Bastress went back to prison and, in time, earned parole once again. In August of 1952, the now forty-two-year-old bandit was arrested in Norristown, along with an accomplice named Charles Stalnaker. The two men pleaded guilty to burglary and larceny charges before Judge E. Arnold Forrest in October and admitting to staging robberies at auction houses in Limerick, Gilbertsville, and Barren Hill. In addition to the punishment for these crimes, Bastress received an additional ten-year sentence for parole violation. Upon the completion of his sentence, he moved to Tabor Avenue in Philadelphia with his wife, but he spent the remainder of his life in ill health. He died on May 20, 1977, at the age of sixty-seven, and was laid to rest at Northwood Cemetery in Philadelphia.

If Donald Bastress had played a role in the 1932 murder of Claude Haas, he never spoke a word of it, and to this day, no one has come forward with evidence positively identifying the killer of the Shamokin Baking Company delivery man. Perhaps this evidence is still waiting to be found somewhere in the woods south of Trevorton, possibly buried beneath the crumbling concrete foundation of an old mule barn.

8

The Lycoming Creek Tragedy

LYCOMING COUNTY

When a small child was found hungry and crying inside an abandoned automobile parked along a rural stretch of Lycoming County in the summer of 1922, the first chapter of a perplexing mystery was written. When the bodies of a man and woman, their throats slashed, were found a few feet away in the waters of Lycoming Creek, the mystery deepened, and to this day, no one knows if Henry Shearer and his wife were victims of a double murder or a murder-suicide.

Early in the evening of Wednesday, July 19, Jeremiah Sayles was driving along the highway near Bodines, eighteen miles north of Williamsport, when his attention was drawn to a vehicle parked along Lycoming Creek. Inside was a young girl of about three years of age. Concerned for the child's safety, Sayles stopped his car and immediately began searching for the child's parents. He saw a portion of a man's clothing protruding from the water and jumped down the embankment for a closer look. What he saw chilled his blood—the body of a man and a woman, partially submerged, a few hundred feet apart. Both of their throats had been cut; one was punctured as if with a knife, the other was slashed from ear to ear. He searched the body of the man for identification and found a watch that had been stopped at nine o'clock. It was now after six in the evening. Witnesses would later come forward stating that they had seen the automobile parked along the creek that morning, but oddly, no one had taken any notice of the little girl crying inside. Sayles also found a

105

small penknife inside the dead man's pocket. The motorist examined the vehicle but found no trace of blood. He found only the remains of the little girl's lunch—orange peels and cookie crumbs. There was no indication of any struggle taking place, and no grass or weeds around the vehicle had been trampled. Only a woman's footprints were found in the mud, near the water's edge. He dragged the bodies from the water onto the bank of the creek, then comforted the weeping child before seeking assistance from nearby farmers.

When Sheriff Thomas Gray arrived, he noted that no jewelry or money was missing. Mrs. Shearer still had on her rings, and $80 was found in her husband's wallet. A Kodak camera was found inside the car; later the film would be developed, showing a smiling couple posing at the creekside. Police identified the couple as Henry and Ruth Shearer of Attica, New York. This was the couple captured on film. The child was their three-year-old daughter, Helen Marie. The Shearers had left their home on Tuesday for a trip to Harrisburg to visit relatives. On Tuesday afternoon, the Shearers visited the home of the dead woman's grandmother, Mary Witherow, in Hornell, New York. They spent two hours in Hornell before continuing on to Troy, where they spent Tuesday night. They resumed their trip in the morning. Henry was employed as a switchman on the Erie Railroad, and the Shearers had been residents of Attica for about six years. Henry had been married once before but sought a divorce after a few months, alleging infidelity. This was all the information that could be gleaned in the early hours of the investigation.

THE GRANDMOTHER'S STORY

On the morning of Friday, July 21, the exhausted child was taken back to her great-grandmother's house in Hornell by train, where she nestled in the old woman's arms, oblivious to the tragedy that left her an orphan. Mrs. Witherow had come to Williamsport by train to identify the bodies, which were resting in a casket at the undertaking parlor of Harold Page on Fourth Street. After she arrived in the city late Thursday night, she told Sheriff Gray an interesting story.

"I dislike to divulge personal sorrows," said the old woman, "but for the sake of my granddaughter I feel that I should. That man whose body lies alongside the woman he killed deserves no sympathy. He lured her to the creek and did away with her." The sheriff did not interrupt. The old woman continued.

"Henry Shearer married my granddaughter four years ago this August in the home of her parents at Hornell. She was Ruth Webb. Her mother and father moved not long ago to California. They seemed to adore one another. Many times after he came home late at night and tired from a hard day spent in firing a locomotive on the Erie Railroad he used to make her get out of bed to play with him. He was like a child that way—always wanting to cut up. He used to tease her about being a year older than he was. Then she would laugh and say, 'Well, I'm still young and won't be twenty-nine until October.' She meant this coming October.

"About four months ago, shortly after they moved to Attica from Buffalo, where they had been living, I noticed Henry acting very strangely. He had lost his former joviality. He flared up at every little thing that didn't suit him. I believed him to be losing his mind. He often returned from work and took great delight in saying nasty things about my granddaughter. Once he told me that if any more children arrived he would not keep them. He told me I could have them. Then he asked his wife to leave him, but she believed the man was run down from overwork. She insisted upon standing by him."

It was shortly after this when Henry instructed his wife to pack her bags and accompany him on a trip to Bachmanville, in Dauphin County, where his parents lived. They had dinner with Mrs. Witherow before they left for Pennsylvania. According to Mrs. Witherow, Henry behaved very strangely during the visit. She tried to convince Ruth to postpone her trip; she told Ruth that Henry didn't seem right—his eyes were "bulging out of his head." Ruth laughed and said that it was just his nerves. A trip to his parents' house would do him good.

"I really believe he intended to kill her when they stopped alongside the creek," the old woman continued. "I believe he posed for his snapshot by the side of the car, then took his wife to the edge of the water and stabbed her to death and committed suicide."

Mrs. Witherow later told reporters in Hornell that Helen Marie had said to her that "Mama was crying when daddy pulled her out of the car," and "Mama's in the water," which seemed to put the mystery of the killer's identity to rest. She added that the other relatives the Shearers had stayed with in Troy thought Henry had been acting strangely.

The Shearer family also came to Williamsport to view the remains, but the father, Abe, was denied permission to see the corpse. "Henry didn't do this," Abe Shearer kept repeating, over and over.

THE MYSTERY DEEPENS

While the public was satisfied with the murder-suicide theory, some had doubts—including the coroner, Dr. George L. Schneider. The coroner's doubts were based on the story told by Mary Witherow to New York reporters. Despite hours of pleading, authorities couldn't get a single word out of the child. If Helen Marie could tell them nothing about what happened when the tragedy was still fresh in her mind, Pennsylvania authorities wondered how and why the child spoke so readily to folks in New York as soon as she got off the train. And, if the dead woman's grandmother and daughter were telling the truth, why was there no evidence of a struggle? Why had the girl remained inside the abandoned automobile instead of waving down a passing motorist? This seemed to suggest to some people that Helen Marie might have feared that she was in danger if she left the car.

Other discrepancies were found in Mrs. Witherow's statements. She had said on record that the automobile was owned by her granddaughter, but Henry Shearer's relatives declared that Henry had bought and paid for it himself. They also refuted the old woman's claim that Henry was depressed and morose. They pointed to the photographs from the camera found at the scene. Didn't they show the couple smiling alongside Lycoming Creek? Why should Henry slash Ruth's throat just moments later?

Henry's brother, Aaron, and their father, Abe, disputed nearly everything Mary Witherow had told police and reporters. They even furnished a letter which Ruth had written to them before the Shearers departed New York. It was in her handwriting; Ruth was fond of writing letters to her husband's family. It read:

Slain Couple and Baby

Mr. and Mrs. Henry Shearer, of Attica, N. Y., slain near Williamsport on their way to visit Mr. Shearer's parents, Mr. and Mrs. A. R. Shearer of Bachmanville, Dauphin county. Their 3-year-old daughter Helen Marie, officers believe was left alone in the small car all Wednesday.
This is the first picture of the slain couple and their child to appear in any newspaper.

Harrisburg Telegraph, July 21, 1922.

Hello All!

We'll be down to see you Wednesday for a vacation of a week or more and hope to spend a happy time. If we have good luck, we'll arrive there early in the day.

As Ever,

Henry, Ruth and Helen Marie

The Shearers stated that Henry and Ruth visited often, and they have never seen the slightest indication of any difficulty between them. Attica's Chief of Police was also a friend of Henry's and flatly denied rumors of marital troubles. He knew Shearer to be a good, sober, industrious man. So what was Mary Witherow's angle?

District Attorney Carl A. Schug had his own questions. He originally believed the murder-suicide theory, but after viewing the photographs for himself, he wasn't so sure. He wondered if the couple had been slain elsewhere, then taken to the spot along Route 14. Police pursued this lead, with officers H. E. Zuber and Romaine Thomas helming the investigation. They quickly uncovered another one of Mrs. Witherow's lies; the Shearers had not spent Tuesday night at a relative's home in Troy as she had claimed but had stayed at a hotel. They had checked out at seven o'clock on Wednesday morning, without eating breakfast.

Residents of Bodines and nearby communities of Trout Run and Ralston came forward with their own theories. Lycoming Creek was popular with fishermen and was fished daily from one end to the other year-round. The rocks upon which the bodies were found were a favorite spot from which anglers cast their lines. The official timeline didn't seem to add up, either. The dead man's watch was stopped at nine o'clock, and Sheriff Gray had found the bodies well after six. Yet, during that time, many claimed to have been in the vicinity of the creek, though no one had alerted the authorities until evening.

Lycoming County locals also scoffed at the idea that the dead man's tiny pocketknife could've been the murder weapon. It simply wasn't large enough nor sharp enough to slash two throats from ear to ear.

According to the coroner, the gash on Ruth's neck was five inches in length, and the edges of the wound were more consistent with an attack from a razor—not a penknife with a dull two-inch blade. However, the wound in Henry's neck had not been a slash but instead a puncture wound. The weapon had left a large hole with jagged edges. The *Harrisburg Telegraph* reported that "the hole in Shearer's neck is large enough for insertion of a medium-sized sponge," and that part of the thorax had been cut away. Could it be that Henry had dulled his knife so much by slashing his wife's throat that he had no choice but to stab himself? The coroner also noted two lumps on Henry's head: one on the front and one on the back. Falling onto a rock might explain one of these lumps, but not both. Another curious fact is that blood was found on Henry's undershirt but not on Ruth's clothing.

A POSSIBLE LEAD

When word of the tragedy reached New York, Rochester's Chief of Police, Fred W. Tepel, received a letter from a resident named M. P. Davis describing an unsettling experience he had while near the scene of the tragedy a few weeks earlier. According to Davis, he had been driving from Rochester to Allenwood, Lycoming County, on July 2 when the driver of a green automobile attempted to rob him below Bodines by backing up to his car in front of a railroad crossing. Davis noted that the car contained three men and a woman and that the two men in the backseat were getting out of the car when Davis made his escape. Davis noted that the vehicle's tag was from Altoona.

But, if robbery had been the motive, why had nothing been removed from the bodies of Mr. and Mrs. Shearer? Were the bandits scared off by an approaching motorist or fisherman before they could take anything valuable? It's possible that the robbers meant to return, perhaps warning the little girl to stay in the car and keep quiet—or else.

Attention also turned to two women hikers who were seen in the vicinity at the time of the tragedy. A special railroad officer had seen the women near the Shearer automobile on Wednesday morning but had thought nothing of it at the time. Why hadn't Helen Marie said anything about the hikers? Had she been sleeping?

On July 24, the funeral of Henry Shearer was held at the home of his parents near Bachmanville, and he was laid to rest at the Spring Creek Church Cemetery near Hershey. Over nine hundred people attended the graveside services. Ruth Shearer's body was returned to Steuben County, New York, and she was buried at Rural Cemetery outside of Hornell.

CONFLICTS AND CONTRADICTIONS

Dr. Fred E. Widdington analyzed the pocketknife found in Henry Shearer's pocket and announced that he had found traces of human blood on

Ruth Shearer. *Buffalo Times*, July 21, 1922.

the blade. Opinion once again shifted back to the murder-suicide theory, though it begged the question—how is it possible for someone to stab himself in the throat and then have the presence of mind to put the knife back in his pocket? Of course, the possibility exists that Shearer had cut himself with the knife at some point predating July 19 and had failed to remove every trace of blood. To answer this question, authorities knew they had to find out everything they could about the pocketknife. When had it been purchased? And where?

It was discovered that, after checking out of their hotel, the Shearer's had stopped at Dobbins' Hardware Store in Troy, where Henry purchased a pocketknife. However, upon studying the knife found inside Henry's pocket, the proprietor declared that it was not the same knife he had sold to Shearer. Witnesses said they'd seen the Shearer automobile passing through Ralston at 8:05, sixty-five minutes after they'd checked out of the hotel in Troy.

THE CASE IS CLOSED

On July 28, Trooper Leo Gratcofsky of the State Police announced that they had closed their investigation. They concluded that Henry Shearer had taken his own life after murdering his wife. Even though facts strongly refuted this theory, it was reported that Gratcofsky had gone to Hornell to speak with Mrs. Witherow. She told the trooper that around Christmas, she had received a letter from Ruth stating that she was "afraid for her life" and asked Mrs. Witherow to come to Attica and stay with her. Strangely, Mary Witherow had never mentioned this detail before.

Mrs. Witherow—whose numerous inconsistencies had been well documented in dozens of newspapers by this time—also told Trooper Gratcofsky that, during her granddaughter's funeral, Helen Marie had noticed a pool of water along the road to the cemetery. According to Mrs. Witherow, the child had looked at the water and said, "Mama drown! Mama drown!" She said that she asked the girl what she meant. "Mama holler! Mama holler!" Helen allegedly replied.

"Why did mama holler?" asked Mrs. Witherow.

"Daddy pushed her," was the reply.

Helen Marie Shearer, the lone survivor of the tragic automobile trip. Philadelphia Evening *Public Ledger*, July 21, 1922.

Even though it would've been circumstantial evidence at best, Gratcofsky asked Mary Witherow to produce this incriminating letter. She could not. She did provide him with another letter, however. It was from Ruth's parents and hinted that Ruth may have been planning a trip to California to visit. At the time of the Lycoming Creek tragedy, Ruth Shearer's mother had already died. So how old was this letter? Apparently, the State Police didn't seem interested enough to find out.

Instead, they spoke with Henry's co-workers and discovered that Henry had been laid off just days earlier. They reached the conclusion that Henry must have been despondent over financial worries. One of the railroad engineers, Addison Gitner, had told Gratcofsky that he feared Henry was going insane. "He would at times jump across the cab of the engine to the engineer's side and cry out that the men were trying to get him," claimed Gitner. He had also once remarked to Gitner that he was "going away" soon. When Gitner asked him what he meant, Shearer said that he was "going to have a new home." While Sheriff Thomas Gray and the district attorney may have scoffed at this "evidence," it was enough for the State Police to declare Henry the perpetrator of a murder-suicide.

There is one strange coincidence attached to the case of the Shearer murders; Sheriff Gray recalled that a few years earlier, another man named Shearer (no relation) had attempted suicide in the Lycoming County jail—by slashing his throat with a penknife.

Mary Witherow passed away on October 3, 1939, at the age of eighty-three, and is buried at Rural Cemetery along with her granddaughter. As for Helen Marie, records show that she lived with Mrs. Witherow up until the time of her great-grandmother's death. Whatever became of her is unclear, although newspapers reported that she had inherited one-quarter of the Witherow estate after the funeral.

Accidental Death Theory

Were Henry and Ruth murdered by would-be robbers? Did Henry, in a fit of insanity, murder his wife at the side of the creek with a pocketknife before taking his own life and falling into the water? These are the prevailing theories, but a careful examination of the timeline shows that a different scenario is entirely possible—a scenario in which Henry died by accident.

The man who found the bodies on the evening of July 19 searched the car and found crumbs on the floor, while the Kodak film revealed that the couple had appeared in the best of spirits just minutes before the terrible tragedy. Mrs. Witherow had told Sheriff Gray about the couple's playful teasing. "He was like a child that way—always wanting to cut up," she had said. "They adored each other." The possibility that the Shearers had stopped alongside Lycoming Creek to eat seems logical, as the facts show that the Shearers left Troy at seven o'clock that morning without eating breakfast. They stopped at Dobbins' Hardware Store, leaving around 7:30. They would've reached Bodines about forty-five minutes later. This corresponds with the sighting of the Shearer automobile in nearby Ralston at 8:05. Helen Marie might have eaten first before returning to the car for a nap, while Henry and Ruth walked down to the rocks with their food. Horseplay may have ensued since Henry was a playful sort of fellow, and Henry might have begun choking. He might have fallen onto a rock, which would account for one of the bumps on his head. Ruth, his adoring wife, may have knelt down and tried in vain to dislodge the bit of food from her husband's throat. She might've begun to panic—help was too far away, and she had to act quickly. Remembering the pocketknife her husband had purchased at the hardware store, Ruth might have attempted an amateur tracheotomy—a relatively bloodless operation when done correctly. If only she could get Henry to breathe again, that would buy her enough time to summon help. But the procedure went wrong; the blood ran back into Henry's throat. He choked to death on his own blood. This would explain the hole in Henry's neck—not a gash or a stab—and why blood was found only on his undershirt.

Overcome by grief and the fear of arrest, she could have returned the knife to Henry's pocket, then dragged him down to the creek, desperately hoping the cold water would revive him—but the water only succeeded in stopping his watch at 9:05. So far, the timeline fits perfectly, and dragging Henry to the water's edge could account for the second bump on Henry's head.

Ruth composed herself and calmly returned to the car. Her little girl was sleeping so peacefully. Surely, someone would come along and take her in, give her a new life, one with a father in it. Ruth left her sleeping girl some cookies and an orange. She may have remembered Henry's shaving razor—what man would leave on a weeklong trip without one? She took the razor and went down to the water's edge (don't forget, the only footprints found along the creek were those of a woman), where she entered the water and joined her beloved husband in death. Perhaps it was out of grief, or perhaps it was because she felt that, without a father, little Helen Marie would be destined to a life of hardship and poverty.

Ruth Shearer must've known that most self-slashings of the throat fail; when the head is thrown back, the jugular vein is virtually unreachable. She knew enough to keep her chin down when she made the slash, thereby ensuring fatal results—and also explaining why there was no blood found on her clothing. Her blood washed downstream, and the razor dropped from her hand into the rushing water, never to be seen again. It all fits, down to the last minute, down to the last detail.

Maybe, just maybe, Abe Shearer had been right all along—his son hadn't killed anyone. Maybe Henry Shearer had been killed accidentally by the woman who was attempting to save his life.

Sadly, Abe had tried valiantly, but in vain, to have Ruth buried alongside her son. The Shearers had welcomed Ruth into their family with open arms, accepting her as one of their own. Not surprisingly, it had been Mary Witherow who had arranged to have her granddaughter's body brought back to Hornell for burial. If the accidental death theory is correct, the saddest part of this tragic, forgotten tale is that husband and wife lay hundreds of miles apart, buried in different states.

9

The Murder of Margaret Martin

WYOMING COUNTY

The leaves had long since fallen, and trapping season was in full swing in Wyoming County in the winter of 1938. Despite the cold December chill, a teenage farm boy eagerly set his muskrat traps along a tiny creek in the sparsely populated wilderness between Keelersburg and Thurston Hollow on a Wednesday afternoon. Beside an abandoned wooden bridge, nineteen-year-old Anthony Rezykowski carefully slid down a steep embankment to reach a spot where his nocturnal prey had worn a muddy trail from his den to the edge of the icy water. But, before Rezykowski had a chance to set his trap, his eyes were drawn to an object which, at first glance, appeared to be the limb of a tree protruding above the water's surface beneath the old bridge. Squinting, he made a shocking discovery: It was a limb, all right, but one not made of wood. He crept a few steps closer and discovered the object poking through the water was a human hand and a few inches of a thin, delicate arm. Although the water was neither swift nor deep, he could only see that the limb was extending from some sort of sack resting on the bottom of the creek.

The youth immediately took off running to the nearest home, a farmhouse occupied by John Kapolka, and the authorities were notified. Coroner Ray W. Greenwood soon arrived on the scene, and the body was taken to Kapolka's home for a preliminary examination before being removed to Greenwood's morgue in Tunkhannock. Before long, Lieutenant Charles Cook of the Pennsylvania Motor Police, accompanied by Corporals Jacob Hess and Joseph Santille, arrived at the morgue, where they were met by several other law enforcement officials and Identification Expert Benjamin Lee. The morgue must've resembled a policeman's convention by late afternoon; the group swelled to include officers Kenneth Tissue, David Greene, Louis Shupnik, and Major William A. Clark, Luzerne County Detective Richard Powell, two assistant county detectives, District Attorney Leon Schwartz of Luzerne County, Assistant District Attorney John Dando, and Kingston Chief of Police David Francis. With so many lawmen in the mortuary, it didn't take long to identify the mutilated body as that of a missing nineteen-year-old Kingston girl named Margaret Martin.

Margaret had been missing for almost four days, which is why so many Luzerne County officials traveled over miles of treacherous, icy roads to Wyoming County to view the body on December 21. Margaret, a graduate of the Wilkes-Barre Business College, was last seen on Saturday morning, December 17, when she left home to meet a man who had telephoned with an offer of employment as a stenographer at an insurance agency. This man, who had given his name as R. P. Davis, asked Margaret to meet him at Kingston Corners because he did not know how to get to her house. No one had seen or heard from the young woman since she had left her home on Covert Street in Kingston at nine o'clock that morning.

THE AUTOPSY

The autopsy was conducted at Greenwood's morgue by Dr. Gordon Guyler, a skilled pathologist from Wilkes-Barre, who was assisted by Dr. Davenport of Tunkhannock. It was long past midnight by the time the autopsy was complete, and both doctors had reached the conclusion that Margaret Martin's death had been caused by strangulation. The body, which was covered in bruises, had been nude when trussed up with hemp rope and placed inside the burlap sack. These bruises indicated that a terrible struggle had taken place before the woman was strangled. Several slash wounds on the body indicated that the killer had tried to cut it into smaller pieces but had given up, his fingers probably numb from the bitter cold. A long slash had been made in her abdomen.

"The condition of the body indicates the girl has been dead some twenty-four hours," said Dr. Guyler, but he admitted that the body's submersion in ice-cold water made it impossible to be certain. One thing of which he was certain, however, was that Margaret had been raped prior to her murder. He later revised his opinion, believing that Margaret had been held captive at an unknown location for three days and that, quite possibly, she had been killed just hours before the teenage trapper found the body.

"It was only an accident that she was found," said Major Clark. "Her body might've lain there twenty years and not been found."

Major Clark was the one who telephoned Margaret's parents and broke the news to the mother, Mrs. John Martin, who had hardly slept since her daughter's disappearance. Margaret's body was transported to Kingston the following day and prepared for burial.

The Martins were an extremely religious family, and inside her bedroom, Margaret kept a shrine devoted to the Virgin Mary. In the days following Margaret's disappearance, her parents, illuminated by the somber glow of candles burning in perpetual sanctuary lamps, had prayed for her return. Neighbors and relatives would also come to this shrine to pray. "I know where Margaret is tonight," said Nellie Martin after she had received the call informing her that the body at the morgue had been identified. "She is with God. I am happy to know that she died as she lived. We will bury her on Christmas Eve, on the eve of the birth of her Divine Savior. She was a true daughter to Him."

The father, John Martin, expressed no hatred toward his daughter's killer. John, a veteran who had been wounded in France during the war yet continued to labor in the coal mines, told reporters, "We do not, and we cannot, want vengeance."

THE DISAPPEARANCE OF MARGARET MARTIN

To describe Margaret Martin as a good girl is an understatement. At her high school graduation, she earned a medal for eleven consecutive years of perfect attendance. She taught Sunday School at St. Ignatius and hadn't missed mass since her first Holy Communion. After graduating from Kingston High School in 1937, Margaret enrolled in business school and graduated with honors on December 1, 1938.

Early on the morning of December 17, a man telephoned Victor Lee Dodson, head of the Wilkes-Barre Business College, stating that his insurance agency was in need of a stenographer. Dodson was asked if he had any recent graduates who might be interested in the position. Dodson gave the caller the name and address of his prize pupil, Margaret. The Martins, who were not affluent by any stretch of the imagination, did not own a phone of their own, and their telephone messages were conveyed to them by a neighbor. Minutes later, the same man called for Margaret from a local pay phone, giving his name as R. P. Davis. He asked her to meet him at the main intersection in town, claiming that he wasn't familiar with the neighborhood and might have difficulty locating her house on Covert Street. Margaret's mother found the phone call suspicious, but Margaret assured her that she would return home shortly. She was going on foot to meet Davis at the busiest intersection in town in broad daylight. What could possibly go wrong?

When noon came and went without her daughter's return, Nellie Martin grew worried. She telephoned friends and neighbors, but none of them had seen the young woman. She called the police, who made a routine investigation, but their search was fruitless. Business owners on Wyoming Avenue and Market Street couldn't recall any customers who matched the woman's description, and there had been no reports of strangers acting in a suspicious manner. But the afternoon was still early, the police said to Mrs. Martin. They, too, were certain that Margaret would be home soon.

"Margaret was very anxious to get work as a stenographer and naturally agreed to meet this party at the corner," said Nellie. "Margaret had never left home overnight before. She had never done any traveling whatsoever."

As the afternoon turned to evening with no word from Margaret, the State Police and local authorities began an intensive search, cruising the streets and alleys of Wilkes-Barre and surrounding communities with their eyes peeled for the pretty brunette teenager. By the following day, Major Clark began to fear the worst. Sex trafficking had been a major

Margaret Martin. *Scranton Times*, December 22, 1938.

issue in Luzerne and Wyoming Counties, and he suspected that Margaret may have been kidnapped for this purpose, though he admitted he didn't have any evidence to support this theory. However, police had recently investigated complaints from three young Kingston women who had answered newspaper advertisements offering office employment, only to discover that it was an offer to work in the sex trade. To Major Clark, it was a familiar story: Traffickers singled out attractive young women from poor, working-class families and offered them glamorous careers on stage or in the movies. They left the region voluntarily with dreams of fame and fortune, only to find themselves working against their will in houses of ill repute.

Detective Richard Powell and his men searched every known brothel and roadhouse in a fifteen-mile radius, on the theory that Margaret might've been held prisoner, but found no trace of the missing teenager. In Scranton, police investigated a report of a young woman fitting Margaret's description who had stood crying outside a local theater, apparently in a state of amnesia. Major Clark broadcast a missing persons alert across nine states, while radio stations broadcasted Margaret's descriptions across Pennsylvania. Major Clark and the 275 troopers under his command ran down every lead as reports poured in, and detectives tirelessly tried to determine the true identity of the man who called himself R. P. Davis.

But everything changed on December 21 with the finding of Margaret's body.

AUTHORITIES OPTIMISTIC
The section between Keelersburg and Center Moreland was well off the beaten track, and the finding of Margaret's body in such a remote area was considered a stroke of good fortune by authorities. It was a desolate region, dotted by a handful of farms and hunting cabins, and the appearance of an unfamiliar face or vehicle might've been remembered by locals. "We didn't know very much before because we had so little to work upon," stated Major Clark. "I believe that, due to weather and road conditions, we will be able to completely isolate the immediate scene of the crime from amateur investigators and from curiosity seekers who

would obliterate any possible clues." Lieutenant Charles Cook, of the Tunkhannock State Police substation, organized an inch-by-inch search of the vicinity, and Major Clark was confident that the killer would soon be caught. But then a winter storm blanketed Wyoming County with three inches of snow, putting a temporary freeze (quite literally) on the search.

However, back in Luzerne County, things were about to get red hot. On December 22, the most important development in the investigation up to that point occurred when three witnesses came forward claiming they had seen Margaret getting into her abductor's automobile on the morning of her disappearance from Kingston Corners. Mr. and Mrs. William Agrafiotis and their daughter, Mary, lived in an apartment overlooking the bustling intersection known as Kingston Corners, where the business school graduate was to meet her prospective employer. The man they saw was around twenty-five or twenty-six years old, dressed in a brown double-breasted business suit, and standing about five feet and eleven inches in height. He had a light complexion and a sturdy build, and he carried himself with the dignified air of someone who had graduated from an institution of higher learning. He was driving a late-model black coupe without a spare tire mounted to the trunk. After a short conversation, the girl reportedly entered the vehicle, and it drove away towards Tunkhannock.

The description of this vehicle tallied with a description given by boys from Keelersburg, who said they had seen a black Pontiac about three hundred feet off the main highway on a back road hours before the body was discovered. The car had heavy-duty tires in the rear and light tires in the front. This led authorities to believe that the owner was probably a resident of one of the hilly sections of Wyoming County, where unpaved roads called for sturdy tires. Troopers also believed that the burlap sack was the kind used for fertilizer, coffee, or chicken feed.

At sunrise on December 23, Lieutenant Cook and his troopers resumed the search for Margaret's clothing, the Kingston High School class ring which was missing from her finger, and other clues. Throughout the morning, snow fell slowly but steadily, but that didn't prevent hundreds of volunteers from joining the search. By afternoon, their numbers were bolstered by members of Battery B, 109th Field Artillery, of the Pennsylvania National Guard. District Attorney Schwartz and his staff also joined the search party.

Wild rumors spread through the region, and even experienced reporters had difficulty separating fact from fiction. Word had it that the killer had been caught in Allentown, while others heard the killer had taken his own life after fleeing into the woods, and still others insisted that the strangler had been killed in a gun battle with State Police. Major Clark shot down each fake story that came along but insisted that his men would have the killer apprehended within twenty-four hours.

THE FUNERAL

It seemed the whole neighborhood had turned up for the wake at the family home and the funeral at St. Ignatius on December 24. During the wake, Margaret was laid out in a pink silk dress, a corsage of purple orchids pinned to her chest. In her left hand she held a rosary, while a spray of nineteen roses—one for each year of her life—lay at her feet. The embalmer had done a superb job concealing Margaret's wounds, which had been rendered invisible to the eye. At ten o'clock, the casket was closed and carried from the Martin home on Covert Street on the shoulders of ten young men. After a solemn requiem mass at St. Ignatius Church, the casket was taken to the parish cemetery on Pringle Hill, just a stone's throw away from the cheerful yellow house where the family had lived until moving into a larger house in Kingston a few years before the tragedy.

Margaret's parents, along with her brother and two younger sisters, watched stoically as the metal casket, engulfed in flowers, was lowered into the grave. They shed no tears, only because that salty reservoir had been exhausted during the tortuous days and nights of the girl's disappearance. Nellie and John's eldest daughter had come home for the holidays but at a cost too terrible for words.

On the day of the funeral, police were looking into a statement given by a girl from nearby Dupont who said that she had been accosted on December 16, the day before Margaret's disappearance, by a man who tried to lure her into his car by claiming that he had been sent by an employment office. The man said that his office had a job lined up for her, but she would have to go with him immediately before it was given to somebody else. The girl grew suspicious when the man wouldn't take no for an answer and fetched her brother, who ordered the stranger to "be on his way." Fortunately, he was able to get the stranger's license plate number. The man in whose name the vehicle was registered lived on a rural road near Bloomsburg, Columbia County. State Police wasted no time in paying him a visit, only to discover that there was no link to the slaying of Margaret Martin.

On Christmas Day, prayers were offered to the Martin family in every Catholic church in the Diocese of Scranton. At the conclusion of the pontifical high mass at St. Peter's Cathedral, Bishop William J. Hafey eulogized the slain teenager as a martyr, a girl who "preferred to lose her temporal life than to soil her soul with deadly sin." Throughout the Wyoming Valley, parents celebrated the holiday by embracing their children tightly and thanking the heavens that their own daughters were safe and sound. One such parent was a state trooper who showed up at the Wyoming barracks on Christmas Day ready to work, even though Major Clark had given his men the holiday off. "When I was home and saw my little girl reading a book in the living room and I realized that she, too, might meet with this fiendish killer, I just couldn't relax," he said to the *Scranton Tribune*. "I had to get back on the job to see what I could do to bring about his arrest."

Meanwhile, in Wyoming County, troopers extended their search area and investigated several cabins around Keelersburg, trying to locate the spot where Margaret had been held captive. Before long, they would strike pay dirt.

A HISTORIC SEARCH AND A SLEW OF COPYCATS

Between Margaret's disappearance on December 17 and Christmas Day of 1938, State Police investigated over one thousand leads in the case. In terms of manpower, the search for Margaret Martin's killer was the largest manhunt on Pennsylvania soil up to that point, with the exception of the hunt for Abraham Lincoln's assassin in 1865. Sadly, the national publicity generated by the case inspired degenerates across the country to emulate

Investigators examine the bridge where the body was found. The man pointing to the water is County Detective Richard Powell. *Scranton Times*, December 22, 1938.

the unknown killer's methods; Major Clark stated that over fifty young women who dodged similar fates had been questioned at the Wyoming State Police barracks alone since Margaret's disappearance. In nearly every case, the methodology was the same: A dapper, smooth-talking gentleman would attempt to lure a pretty girl into his automobile with an offer of employment. While this technique had long been used by "white slavers" (as sex traffickers were known back then), it was Margaret's killer who honed it to deadly perfection. This gave troopers and detectives an added incentive to catch the culprit; every day that went by without his capture only emboldened other would-be abductors. Each day without a resolution meant the possibility of more families ripped apart by tragedy. The next Margaret Martin could be anyone's daughter.

Proof of this took place in Kingston on December 30, when thirty-two-year-old Lyle Maithew was captured after a high-speed chase in which police fired sixteen shots at the suspect's vehicle. Earlier that evening, Maithew had driven up to two girls and tried to lure them into his car. They escaped by hopping on a trolley to Wilkes-Barre, only to find Maithew waiting for them when they hopped off. The girls called the police, who soon spotted the vehicle and gave chase. Sergeant Fred Hinkle of the Kingston Police Department had to resort to his billy club to subdue Maithew, who was hauled by ambulance to the hospital, where he was treated for head injuries. A hunting knife was found inside the vehicle.

To prevent this sort of criminal behavior from becoming a trend, it was necessary to capture Margaret's killer as soon as possible. No leads went uninvestigated, and no stones were left unturned. The burlap sack was sent to a laboratory for chemical analysis. If the sack had been used to store chicken feed or fertilizer, it could point investigators in a rural direction, while coffee or some other pricier commodity might direct the search to Scranton or Wilkes-Barre. A chemical analysis of the contents of the dead girl's stomach was also performed. Dr. Gordon Guyler had already determined that Margaret hadn't eaten since the night before her disappearance. A more thorough analysis might be able to pin down the time of her death to a more accurate degree.

Major Clark also traveled to Moyamensing Prison in Philadelphia to take a three-page statement from an inmate who had told the prison warden that he knew who killed "the Martin girl." John Vickers, a fifty-one-year-old convict, was transported to the Wyoming barracks by automobile and put through an intense grilling. At the time of Vickers' arrest for a parole violation, police had found in his pocket a list containing the names of twenty-five women, which he had obtained from a man named Edwards. Some of the names were those of girls from Luzerne and Wyoming Counties. Ultimately, police were unable to establish any connection between Vickers and Margaret Martin, and police never revealed what the list was for, though some speculated that Vickers had been taking orders for contraceptives, which were illegal at the time.

A DISCOVERY IN FORKSTON
A major break in the case came on December 29, when a pair of footprints in the frozen mud, one made by a man and the other by a woman,

were discovered on the property of James Kerr, near a sawmill in a remote wilderness region near Forkston, about eighteen miles from the spot where Margaret's body was discovered. The woman's footprints accompanied the man's footprints up to a certain point, after which only the man's footprints appeared. Where the woman's footprints had stopped abruptly was a track in the mud, signifying that something heavy had been dragged over the ground.

Incinerated remnants of what appeared to be clothing were found inside the firebox of the sawmill's boiler, and it was theorized that the killer had attempted to cremate the victim's body before being frightened away by a gunshot fired by the sawmill's owner. On the evening of Margaret's disappearance, James Kerr and his wife had heard the sound of steam coming from the safety valve of the boiler, and Kerr raced outside to see a man stuffing material into the firebox. Kerr then fired a warning shot to scare off the trespasser. This shot attracted the attention of a deputy game warden, M. B. Wells, who raced to the mill to investigate. It was Kerr and Warden Wells who found the two sets of footprints in the mud. Near the boiler they found signs of a struggle, with only the man's footprints leading away from the mill.

Major Clark announced that he was "quite positive" that his troopers had finally located the scene of the murder. Police believed that the killer had dragged Margaret's still-warm body to the car before driving to a tannery in Noxen, a rural community eleven miles north of Kingston, where the body was tied up and placed into the burlap sack. This was based on bits of tanbark found inside the sack. However, Clark stated the bark may have been carried by the creek from a tannery upstream from the wooden bridge. In either situation, the victim was most likely dead within twelve hours of leaving home. Clark dispatched a detail of twelve troopers to comb the area for additional clues, instructing them to search every shack and cabin where Margaret may have been held prisoner. On the porch of a nearby cabin owned by Charles Lacey Terry, a funeral director and state representative from Wyoming County, troopers found empty burlap sacks similar to the one the killer had used. Terry told police that the sacks had been on his porch since December 1, when he dropped off bags of coal he had purchased in Nicholson. Police made a close comparison of the material and announced the killer's sack hadn't come from the cabin. Representative Terry, who had followed the case closely, believed that the killer was a local man.

The victim's father, however, believed that the killer was not a resident of the Wyoming County backwoods but, instead, someone much closer to home. "When the slayer is identified and captured, it will be a man all of us have known," predicted John Martin. He insisted that his daughter was too cautious to have gotten into a stranger's car. "That's why we believe this man is someone she had seen before," he added. "She left the house without eating breakfast." Police did not share the same opinion; one of their leading suspects, it was later reported, had been the youth who found the body.

As the year drew to a close, twenty-eight-year-old Robert Bartell of Scranton told police that he saw three young men acting suspiciously around a campfire at a strip mine the day before Margaret's disappearance. The men had a burlap bag. At the State Police substation in Peckville, Bartell was shown photographs of Anthony Rezykowski and his trapper friend, Chester Visniski. Bartell told Lieutenant John Tomek they resembled two of the men he had seen that evening.

GRASPING AT STRAWS

In the fervor to bring the case to a close, authorities made "persons of interest" out of anyone whose actions seemed out of place or unusual, or anyone who had even the most tenuous connection to Margaret Martin. On January 3, 1939, newspapers reported that police had been searching for a middle-aged eccentric farmer who lived near the creek where the body was found. Though this man was a business owner and respected member of the community, his eccentric behavior threw up a red flag. Unknown to the farmer, police had been tracking his movements for days. Police also rechecked with the Wilkes-Barre Business School to see if any additional names of students had been given to the killer. Myrna Stair, a secretary, informed investigators that a second teenage girl from Kingston had been recommended to the mysterious caller. Police tailed this girl for several days in the unlikely event that the killer would strike again in the same town. Police also sought information on any young men who had ever expressed a romantic interest in the victim, and they even checked the guest lists of every party Margaret had attended during the last year of her life. In Scranton, a traveling salesman from Salt Lake City named Paul Rhodine was picked up for questioning after he was accused of writing unsolicited letters to scores of local women while in the area. After providing bus ticket stubs showing that he was in Texas at the time of the Keelersburg slaying, Rhodine was released.

If the State Police seemed to be grasping at straws, it was because their best "clues" had gone up in smoke; the ashes recovered from Kerr's sawmill had been analyzed and were found to contain only waste material. The footprints seen by Kerr and the deputy game warden were probably those of a couple who had used the sawmill to illegally dispose of their household trash. The reason only the man's footprints extended past the mill was probably because the couple had been frightened away by Kerr's warning shot, causing them to run in different directions. The origin of the burlap sack, which Major Clark believed would be easy to trace, remained undetermined. Every cabin, shack, shanty, barn, and abandoned building within a thirty-mile radius of Keelersburg had been searched for clues. The men who had terrorized local girls by trying to lure them into their automobiles were found to have no connection to the Martin case. Major William A. Clark, the State Police commandant who boldly predicted an arrest in twenty-four hours, had nothing to show for his bravado but egg on his face. When questioned by reporters on January 4 about the progress of the investigation, Clark admitted there were no new developments. As the investigation stretched into its third week, even John Martin began losing his patience. Thanks to the nationwide publicity of the case, he and his wife were receiving large batches of mail each day, with many of the letters vulgar and threatening in nature. Perhaps as a means of preserving his sanity, he returned to his job in the mines for the first time since his daughter's disappearance.

THE CHICKEN MAN SQUAWKS

One of the more interesting persons of interest in the Martin case was a thirty-four-year-old poultry dealer from Upstate New York named Frank Mozda. On January 16, Mozda was arrested in Rockland County for attempted sexual assault. It was soon learned that he was a leading suspect in several similar cases in New Jersey and that his parents lived about forty miles north of Kingston in the Lackawanna County village of Simpson. While being interrogated by Detective William Sterns of Rockland County, Mozda admitted to attacking roughly a dozen girls in the vicinity of Simpson in early December of 1938. In questioning Mozda about the attacks on Pennsylvania girls, Sterns asked, "Did you kill one of them?" Mozda hesitated.

"Yes, I did," replied Mozda. "I killed a girl once. I didn't attack her. I killed her, though. I hacked her up pretty much with a hatchet." He then confessed to putting her body into a burlap sack and dumping it in the Lackawanna River. "No, it wasn't the Martin girl," he added. Mozda denied having anything to do with Margaret's disappearance and murder, but Rockland County officials promptly notified authorities in Pennsylvania.

Major Clark was in Harrisburg attending the inauguration of newly elected governor Arthur James when he received word of Mozda's confession. He ordered a full investigation and learned that Mozda had an outstanding warrant in Lackawanna County for non-payment of support to his wife, Nellie. Otherwise, his record was as clean as a whistle. Despite his confession, no women in Pennsylvania had formally accused Mozda of anything. After deserting his wife, he enlisted in the army and left the service at the expiration of his term with an honorable discharge and the rank of sergeant. Constable Dubill of Simpson told state troopers that, aside from abandoning his wife (they eventually made up and got back together), Mozda bore an excellent reputation in the community. Confounding matters, Dubill declared that no body had been pulled from the Lackawanna River, which was only about two feet deep in that area.

The body of the woman Mozda confessed to killing was never found, and several of his own accusers failed to pick him out of a police lineup in New York (though two women identified him as the man they saw hiding behind a bush). The attempted assault charges against him were dismissed. So, what made him confess to a crime that could've sent him to the electric chair? Experts claimed that Mozda had manufactured his crimes purely for the publicity. He died from a heart attack in 1960, at the age of fifty-six, while fishing at Lake Kanawauke in New York. He left behind a wife, two children, and zero major criminal convictions.

J. Edgar Hoover Gets Involved

In late January, it was reported that troopers had successfully traced the burlap sack from a stripe woven into the material. The bag had come from the Great Lakes Cooperative Store in Tunkhannock. Unfortunately, the store had sold hundreds of bags of chicken feed in such a sack between 1930 and 1936. A local farmer reported that he had saved five hundred of these sacks, which he then traded for coal in Forty Fort. The coal company in Forty Fort had used them for deliveries, but they saved each sales receipt. Though it would prove to be a mind-numbing task, police carefully studied all five hundred receipts, to no avail.

Investigators Examine Bag in Which Killer Left His Girl Victim

A major clue in the fiendish slaying of Margaret Martin is the bag in which her trussed, mutilated body was found. The bag, five feet long, two feet wide, is of the variety used in transporting fertilizer or coffee. Shown examining it are, left to right: Lieut. Charles Cook, State Motor Police; Richard Powell, chief of Luzerne County Detectives; Major William A. Clark, commandant of the State Motor Police at Wyoming, and John A. Dando, assistant Luzerne County district attorney.

Scranton Tribune, December 23, 1938.

The lack of progress in the investigation compelled many Pennsylvania residents to appeal to the federal government to intervene. Because John Martin received threatening letters through the US mail, these threats were a federal crime, and J. Edgar Hoover announced his active participation in the historic manhunt for Margaret's killer. On January 22, John Martin signed an agreement with the Federal Bureau of Investigation allowing them to confiscate all mail delivered to the Martin home. This mail was forwarded to FBI headquarters in Washington. Meanwhile, a reward of $1,500 was offered by the Kingston borough for information leading to the arrest of Margaret's killer. No reward was offered by the county commissioners, however.

THE RAUNCHY RESTAURATEUR

On February 4, newspapers reported that Detective Powell of Luzerne County had the "number one suspect" in custody and that an arrest in the Martin case was imminent. The suspect, twenty-seven-year-old Lyle Gordy (alias Danny Russell) of Baltimore, had been one of the co-owners of the One-O-Nine Restaurant in Wilkes-Barre at the time of the Martin murder. In October of 1938, Gordy drove a nightclub dancer from Wilkes-Barre to a point in Wyoming County eight miles from Keelersburg, where he beat her severely. He was arrested but released on bail, and his court date was set for January. On December 18—the day after Margaret was abducted—Gordy fled to Maryland.

Coincidentally, Gordy was also involved in an attempted sexual assault that occurred just three hundred feet from the Martin home. That August, Gordy made a date with a waitress from Kingston, and he drove her to West Dallas, where he attempted to sexually assault her. The waitress was able to escape but not before Gordy punched her in the face. He attempted another sexual assault that October in a Wilkes-Barre parking lot. This victim was able to escape by burning Gordy's hand with a lit cigarette. After Gordy was arrested in Baltimore and returned to Luzerne County to face the music, Detective David Green of the Pennsylvania Motor Police suspected that he might be the man who killed Margaret. Gordy, however, was able to provide an iron-clad alibi for his whereabouts from December 17 to December 21.

Gordy was later convicted and sentenced to seven-and-a-half to twenty years in the Eastern Penitentiary for rape. At the end of his trial, immediately after the jury found him guilty, Gordy lunged at Detective Green and had to be subdued by court officials.

Though some still include Lyle Gordy as one of the top suspects in the unsolved murder of Margaret Martin, there are clear differences in the personalities of Gordy and the Keelersburg killer. Quite simply, a girl like Margaret would not have been his "type." Gordy was the spoiled and entitled son of a prominent Baltimore physician and the type who preferred exotic dancers over stenographers and barmaids over business school grads. Gordy was a hot-headed city slicker who loved the night-life—not at all the type of person who would get up early in the morning to make an appointment with his virginal victim, stuff her into a burlap sack from a Tunkhannock feed store, and drive on an abandoned logging trail to hide the body in a place where only a muskrat trapper would find it. Such a scheme would require planning and methodological thinking, the hallmark of a left-brained individual. Gordy's actions align more with an individual who's right-brain dominant. Margaret's killer was an early bird, which is a trait more associated with left-brain dominant individuals, whereas night owls like Gordy tend to be more right-brained.

COOKE TAKES COMMAND

While Gordy was being grilled by detectives, Major William A. Clark was battling a serious illness that eventually sidelined him for a lengthy period of time. Taking his place was Lieutenant C. S. Cooke. Unlike his predecessor, Cooke promised no prompt arrests or speedy resolution. He played his cards close to his vest, not giving anything away to the bevy of reporters who pestered him at every turn for updates on the investigation. "The status of the case is no different today than it was a month ago," he stated to the press after taking command of the Wyoming barracks.

By February, the Martin family had all but given up hope. Even the sanctuary candles atop Margaret's bedroom altar had been extinguished. "We are sure the police are doing all they can to find the man who took her," said Nellie Martin. "But no matter what they do, they cannot bring

Margaret back to us alive." The victim's aunt, Mrs. William Martin, was blunter in her assessment of the handling of the case.

"We know less about the activities of the police than everyone else," she said to the Hazleton Plain Speaker. "They tell us to have faith in them, but so far there is little to have faith in. The murderer should be caught. For all we know he may be walking around the streets planning another crime. No one can feel safe while he is still at large." The family not only stopped talking about the investigation to the press, but they also stopped speaking to each other. "We do not talk about it anymore," continued Margaret's aunt. "It does no good and only causes more heartaches."

Like many residents of Kingston, Margaret's aunt believed that perverts and degenerates would only be emboldened by law enforcement's failure to apprehend her niece's killer. Statistics show that she was correct. Judge Michael McDonald noted a dramatic increase in morals cases in the county since the abduction and slaying of Margaret Martin. In the span of two months, the Luzerne County grand jury had indicted a total of sixty-two persons—twenty-four of whom were indicted on sex crime charges. Of these cases, seven involved victims from the same township in which the Martins lived. Unless there was something in the Kingston water supply turning men into sex-crazed reprobates, it would seem that sex offenders felt they could enact their crimes without fear of retribution.

In a strange twist of events, John Martin retired from his job as mine foreman in February and took a new position as a guard at the Luzerne County Jail. The reason behind this career change is unclear. Surely, the new position paid less and the commute was longer. Perhaps the job was less physically demanding, or perhaps he had been motivated by the State Police's lack of progress—maybe, as a prison guard, he might overhear a snippet of conversation that would lead to the solution of the case. Loose lips can not only sink ships, but they can also lead to lengthy prison sentences and the electric chair.

Major Cooke's first serious foray into the investigation resulted in the questioning of a thirty-five-year-old Wyoming County man who was picked up on April 10 on information supplied by a Scranton woman who had accompanied him on an impromptu trip to Georgia.

The woman, whose name was not disclosed by authorities, said she had arranged to meet the man in Kingston on the morning of December 17, 1938. The man failed to show up but met with her later that night and proposed a trip to New Jersey and later to Georgia. The man had made unwanted advances toward her in Georgia, so she left him there and raced back to Scranton in his car. When the man returned to Pennsylvania a few days later, she became fearful and told her story to the police. Though the man was thoroughly questioned by detectives, he was able to provide an alibi. When the alibi checked out, the man was released, and the investigation was right back to where it had started.

DISTRICT ATTORNEY REFUSES TO OFFER REWARD

There were no further developments in the case that spring, but the murder was still a leading topic of conversation and debate in Luzerne and Wyoming Counties. In late June, after a *Wilkes-Barre Times* reporter asked District Attorney Schwartz if he had planned to direct the county commissioners to offer a reward for the killer's capture, Schwartz replied that the thought hadn't crossed his mind. "There are too many angles to consider before the district attorney's office makes such a move," said Schwartz. "I feel that I must first review the case and the investigation with police officials."

John MacGuffie, chairman of the county commissioners, offered a rebuttal in which he said that he would be happy to offer a reward if only the district attorney would ask. After all, it was up to Schwartz to decide the reward amount and to determine the conditions of the reward. Schwartz's refusal created a firestorm, but the district attorney believed that offering a reward would inspire law enforcement to wrap up the investigation prematurely or, worse, drop the case entirely. Why should the State Police continue to use up valuable time and resources doing the same work that justice-minded locals and amateur sleuths would be willing to do for free? "I have not asked the county commissioners to offer a reward for the slayer of the Martin girl for the reason that the investigation has not been concluded," he explained. "There is nothing to report on the investigation. When the officers have exhausted every available means to capture the murderer or murderers, I may decide to ask the commissioners to offer a suitable reward."

Colonel Cecil M. Wilhelm, deputy commissioner of the State Police, sensed the district attorney's frustration at the slow progress and lack of arrests and issued a statement on behalf of law enforcement. "It is a case of eliminating a large number of people who might've done this, rather than to charge anyone with anything right away," said Wilhelm. "When the case is solved—and I'm confident it will be—I believe we will all be surprised at the simplicity of the whole operation."

Public sentiment was strongly against District Attorney Schwartz's decision, however well-intentioned, and he agreed to hold a conference with county officials about offering a reward. It was the victim's father and brother who pressured Schwartz during a two-hour conversation with the district attorney and Detective Powell. "The case has reached the point where I am satisfied that the man who killed my daughter was known to her and is also probably known to me," John Martin said to Schwartz. "I believe that the offering of a reward may be the means of releasing information which is now being concealed." Despite Schwartz's reassurances to the Martin family, no reward was offered.

THE KUDZINSKI BROTHERS

There was no shortage of young female sex crime victims in 1939, and any time such crimes occurred in the Wyoming Valley, a possible connection to Margaret Martin was sought by detectives. In August, two brothers from Northmoreland Township with extensive criminal records were arrested on a farm, just a few miles from Keelersburg. Nineteen-year-old John Kudzinski and his twenty-one-year-old brother, Barney, had fled from Luzerne County on June 4 after sexually assaulting two teenage girls from Port Griffith. After hiding out in New York for a while, the brothers returned to Pennsylvania, convinced that the "heat" was off.

On the evening of August 3, Trooper Arthur V. Jones traced the Kudzinskis to the farm in Center Moreland, and they were taken into custody without incident. Though authorities could find no connection between the brothers and Margaret, it was learned that the brothers were experienced criminals; they were convicted of breaking and entering and larceny at a West Wyoming store in early 1938, while Barney had served a six-month sentence in 1935 for stealing a car. The statutory rape case came before Judge Jones, who dealt the Kudzinski brothers two-and-a-half- to five-year sentences. Though it is unlikely that John and Barney had anything to do with Margaret's abduction and murder, it is not entirely impossible; they would have been out of jail from the larceny conviction and living in the vicinity of the crime at the time of Margaret's murder.

THE BOXER

On Friday, August 21, a teacher from Forty Fort named Charles Wesley Schooley was arrested for assaulting a twenty-three-year-old-woman in Kingston. Schooley, who had previously taught school in Hanover Township but was teaching at a public school in Cambria County at the time of the incident, had been on the boxing team while a student at Penn State and was known to have a hot temper. On the day of the incident, Schooley approached the young woman in his car and ordered her to get inside. When she refused, Schooley said, "Remember the Martin case? Get into the car." She obeyed, and Schooley drove to a secluded spot, where he allegedly beat and forced himself upon the victim. According to the victim, whose name was not released by police to protect her identity, he had mentioned Margaret Martin's name several times during the attack.

Schooley was arraigned on rape and sodomy charges, and his preliminary hearing was held on September 19. During his trial on October 3, the testimony was so graphic and disturbing in nature that Judge John J. Aponick ordered all spectators out of the courtroom. Despite the mounds of evidence produced by the prosecution, Schooley was acquitted on the two morals charges but found guilty of a lesser offense. He was ordered to pay a fine of $100 and released. Though it was entirely possible, and likely probable, that Schooley had been in Kingston around the time of the Martin murder (he often returned home to Luzerne County during holidays and school vacations), no evidence was uncovered linking him to the crime.

Ace Sleuth Called onto Case

After ten months of investigation and very little to show for it, State Police Commissioner Lynn G. Adams addressed concerns about the case. "We're making some progress," stated Colonel Adams. "At least we're finding out who didn't commit the murder." On October 13, Adams assigned one of the Pennsylvania Motor Police's top detectives to the Martin case full time. The detective, whose identity was kept secret, was granted authority to resort to "every scientific device for crime detection" and given access to FBI forensic laboratories. "We don't solve 'em all but our average is as good as anybody's," said Adams, who pointed out that the turning point in murder investigations frequently occurs after a long cooling-off period, when the perpetrator lets his guard down. Adams hinted that troopers were still watching "two or three" suspects in the Wilkes-Barre area. Unfortunately, the year drew to a close without any further developments.

A Curious Confession

In September of 1942, a New York City man named Orban Taylor was picked up on the streets of Scranton for public drunkenness. Taylor, who had once lived in Wilkes-Barre, was living the life of a vagrant ever since his dishonorable discharge from the army. While in custody, the twenty-one-year-old man was identified as the person who, just days earlier, had forcefully detained a Wilkes-Barre woman in his hotel room at knifepoint before sexually assaulting her. The woman claimed that Taylor had choked her with a towel and threatened to kill her if she notified the police.

In his inebriated state at police headquarters, Taylor confessed to knifing a man, staging five robberies in New York, defrauding hotels in Philadelphia, kidnapping a woman in Newark, assaulting a girl in New York, escaping from a military prison, and a litany of other crimes. Then he confessed to killing Margaret Martin. Police were skeptical of Taylor's claims, but when he continued to speak of details that only someone familiar with the case would know, Major Clark and Captain of Detectives George Donaldson were called to the police station. Taylor made a detailed confession, but at the end of his twenty-hour questioning, he broke down and recanted his story. Major Clark believed that Taylor was delusional, but Scranton police sent queries to New York authorities and the War Department in Washington to see if any part of his story checked out.

It was soon learned that Taylor was telling the truth about some of his previous crimes. He had abducted fourteen-year-old Delores Davis from Central Park and kept her prisoner in his hotel room for three weeks. She hadn't been seen since Taylor dropped her off in New Jersey. Captain Donaldson had been informed by the War Department that Taylor was committed to the guardhouse at Fort Jay, Governor's Island, on November 10, 1939, where he was to serve an eighteen-month sentence. He escaped on October 20, 1940, and was recaptured on November 27. He was dishonorably discharged on August 15, 1941. And while Taylor was stationed at Fort Jay during the time of the Martin murder, it appeared that he was on leave for the holidays. If authorities could place Orban Taylor in the Wyoming Valley on or around December 17, 1938, it would be the biggest break in the investigation thus far. But no such connection could be established, and the investigation hit a serious snag when Taylor couldn't accurately describe Margaret's clothing or jewelry or what had become of these items after the slaying.

Taylor was remanded to the Luzerne County Jail, where he remained until October 3, when Judge Thomas F. Farrell signed extradition papers allowing New York authorities to take him back to answer to the charges in the Delores Davis case. Taylor pleaded with Judge Farrell to be sentenced in Luzerne County, as the charges there were not as serious as those pending in New York. Taylor was assured that, if New York failed to send him to jail, Luzerne County prosecutors would be happy to finish the job. Taylor was sentenced to the Elmira Reformatory, where he died in 1944 after drinking typewriter cleaning fluid that he had mistaken for alcohol.

The Case Goes Cold

The false confession of Orban Taylor marked the last serious development in the Martin case. Though other persons of interest would be questioned, none were seriously considered as suspects. The killer most

certainly had to have been a local, as the bridge was on a disused con-
necting road between Thurston Hollow and the main state road between
Keelersburg and Center Moreland. Several years before the murder, this
road had been relocated, leaving the bridge abandoned about one hundred yards off the highway, which, by 1938, had become overgrown with
brush and scarcely visible. Quite simply, an out-of-towner would not
have been able to locate it.

On the one-year anniversary of Margaret's death, the *Scranton Tribune* reported that three hundred suspects had been questioned or held
under surveillance since the beginning of the investigation, most of their
names never released to the public. One name that got leaked out, however, was that of Leo Curry, a twenty-six-year-old nightclub entertainer
who was sentenced to a year in jail by Judge M. F. McDonald for selling
and taking orders for contraceptives. In court, he testified that he had
been questioned as a suspect in the Martin case. This claim was denied
by State Police. Nonetheless, Curry's testimony gave rise to a persistent
rumor which has never been proven or disproven—that Margaret Martin
may have been pregnant, or worried that she may become pregnant, at
the time of her murder.

Could it be possible that Margaret had been involved in a secret
relationship and had used the job interview as a ruse to meet a lover?
This might explain why the rendezvous took place in broad daylight in
a public place, or why Margaret had skipped breakfast that morning.
Perhaps she had left her home expecting a romantic breakfast at a local
tearoom but discovered—much too late—that her lover had a different
destination in mind. Might it be possible that Margaret had been obtaining contraceptives from John Vickers (the Moyamensing inmate arrested
with a lengthy list of women's names) or Leo Curry? Perhaps, with both
men hiding from the law, she had become pregnant and wanted to meet
her paramour to break the news, which led him to murder.

This is, of course, a far-fetched theory, yet it does make sense when
one considers the following facts: The caller knew that Margaret's
mother might answer the telephone, which is why he used an alias.
When told about the phone call by her daughter, Nellie Martin found
the story highly suspicious, but Margaret assuaged her by saying that

she'd be home shortly. Margaret's abdomen had been slashed by the killer's knife, which obviously has some psychological significance. State police searched for the guest lists from every social function Margaret had attended in the twelve months leading up to her death, and while police may have publicly denied that Curry was a "suspect" in the murder, that doesn't mean that he was not questioned about other matters involving the victim. These facts suggest that the State Police may have been working on the pregnancy theory but had chosen not to divulge this information to the public out of respect for the victim's family. It is unclear whether or not the coroner who performed the autopsy would be able to detect an early-stage pregnancy in 1938. Unfortunately, since autopsy reports are expressly exempt from Pennsylvania's Right-to-Know Law, the truth of the matter may never be known.

Oddly, or perhaps fittingly, the name of the long-forgotten victim endures in the topography of Northmoreland Township; near the spot where the body was found, there is a Margaret Hollow Road and a stream known as Martin Creek.

10

The Evil Eye Killer

PHILADELPHIA COUNTY
Founded in 1683 by Quakers and Mennonites who fled Europe to avoid religious persecution, the Philadelphia neighborhood of Germantown has a long and impressive history. Germantown is perhaps best known as the site of a major Revolutionary War battle that resulted in a British victory and the Continental Army's subsequent retreat to Valley Forge under George Washington, but it was also the birthplace of the abolitionist movement in America. Just five years after the founding of Germantown, leading citizens presented a petition to the Quaker church calling for the banning of slavery. Drafted in 1688 by the town's founder, Francis Pastorius, this document was the first anti-slavery petition in the Thirteen Colonies. Today, dozens of historical sites and painstakingly preserved buildings from the Colonial Era help tell the story of our nation's founding and Germantown's prominent role in shaping American history.

One of the darker chapters of Germantown history, however, was written in 1932 with the bizarre murder of a Mennonite church leader named Norman Bechtel. There are many curious details about Bechtel's unsolved murder, but what makes this case particularly strange is that the killer carved strange symbols into the face of the victim, which, according to some, linked the murder to an occult ritual.

The Judge's Dog Walker and the Trolley Motorman

A few minutes before midnight on January 19, Patrolman Rudolph Lehman hopped off the trolley at Wayne and Wiconisco Avenues. Though most of Germantown was sleeping soundly, Patrolman Lehman's workday was just getting started. Near the Stokes estate, Patrolman Lehman used a police call box to report to duty, officially beginning his shift guarding the home of a judge who had been receiving death threats, presumably from one of the many hardened criminals he had sent to prison. Hanging up the telephone, Patrolman Lehman noticed an automobile emerging from Lone Oak, as the estate of the late Thomas Pym Cope Stokes was known. He thought it strange, as the stately home had been vacant since Mrs. Stokes moved to Delaware County, but not strange enough to distract him from his assignment. The officer's observational instincts, however, had compelled him to look at the driver, and though it was dark, he could see only one person inside the long dark-colored sedan.

Satisfied that nothing was amiss, Patrolman Lehman crossed Westview Avenue and quietly entered the home of Judge Harry McDevitt. It was ten minutes after midnight when he took the judge's dog, Teddy, out for a walk. While passing the Stokes estate, the policeman heard a groan, and he followed the disconcerting sound onto the property and up the driveway. Patrolman Lehman had proceeded about twenty-five feet, to a point between the stable and the rear of the house, when he found a man bleeding profusely on the ground beneath the bare, spreading branches of a cherry tree. Patrolman Lehman called for an ambulance, but the man was unconscious by the time it arrived. He searched the man's pockets for identification, but the wallet was missing. The bleeding stranger was rushed to Germantown Hospital, where he died at 1:55 a.m. without regaining consciousness.

Shortly before Patrolman Lehman discovered the mortally wounded man, the motorman of a passing trolley heard a woman's chilling scream, followed a moment later by the sound of an automobile speeding down Wissahickon Avenue near the Lone Oak estate. The trolley motorman was so startled that he notified the police. He said that two men were inside the vehicle, but that he was unable to obtain the license plate number on account of the darkness. He was otherwise able to provide police with a description of the vehicle.

THE VICTIM IDENTIFIED

It was soon learned that the victim was thirty-one-year-old Norman R. Bechtel, a widely known Mennonite church worker who was returning home from a religious meeting at the home of Reverend D. J. Unruh in Lansdale, seventeen miles north of Germantown. The purpose of the meeting was to discuss plans to hold a three-day summer retreat of young churchgoers at a camp near Quakertown. At the meeting, Norman was elected treasurer of the Young Peoples' Retreat Committee of the Eastern District, Mennonite Conference. He left the meeting with seventeen dollars in his pocket, which comprised the funds of the committee. Norman was seen at around 11:15 p.m. dropping off Robert Ross, superintendent of the First Mennonite Church, at his home on Sparks Street. According to Ross, Norman's alleged girlfriend, Eleanor Temple, had accompanied them to Lansdale.

Since Norman Bechtel was so widely known in the community, it was easy for authorities to gather information about his life and activities. Born to merchant Samuel B. Bechtel in the tiny village of Congo, Norman was a member of a well-known Berks County family. After his father's death, he moved to the borough of Bally, near Boyertown, before coming to Philadelphia to work as an accountant for his uncle, Joseph Bechtel. By night, he attended the Pierce Business College at Temple University. Upon graduating in 1925 with a degree in commerce, Norman accepted a position with the insurance brokerage firm of E. K. Schultz on Walnut Street. He lived with his aunt and uncle, Mr. and Mrs. Joseph Bechtel, in Germantown until 1930, when he moved into the Paramount Court Apartments at 2116 West Venango Street, about four miles south of the Stokes estate. He was unabashedly zealous in his spiritual life; in addition to being president of the Christian Endeavor Society, he maintained an active leadership role at the Mennonite church in Bally and was also a member of the board of directors of the Old Folks Mennonite Home near Schnecksville. In addition to his church work, he was also active in the Boy Scouts, commanding a troop near his home. Norman was also

NORMAN R. BECHTEL

Allentown Morning Call, January 22, 1932.

in charge of the Bechtel Family Association, which held annual reunions in Berks County.

A Perfect Circle of Stab Wounds, An Imperfect Circle of Theories

According to physicians, Norman Bechtel had been stabbed at least twenty times by a long, thin knife, perhaps a dagger or a stiletto, with two of the thrusts piercing his heart. Eight of the stab wounds were in the vicinity of Norman's chest and, strangely, formed a perfect circle six inches in diameter around the heart. The victim's face was battered and slashed, and one of his eyes had been gouged out. There were bruises on the knuckles and forearms. But it was Patrolman Lehman who first noticed the most unusual injury: The victim's cheekbones, forehead, and temples bore strange slashes in the shape of a human eye. These gashes, to Lehman, appeared symbolic in nature.

Detective Warren Murphy was assigned to the case, and his first order of business was to investigate the crime scene. In the rear of the vacant Stokes home, he discovered tire marks indicating that Norman had parked his car there shortly before being ambushed. Based on the victim's injuries, Detective Murphy believed there had to have been two or three attackers. A bloody three-inch piece of pipe was located under some leaves, but this pipe, detectives decided, was too small to have been the murder weapon. The motive for the killing was unclear; though the attackers had stolen Norman's car and yellow pigskin wallet, the seventeen dollars he had been given by the Young Peoples' Retreat Committee had been found inside the dead man's coat pocket at the hospital. The Stokes estate showed no signs of forced entry or recent habitation. Working on the theory that Norman's assailants had kidnapped his girlfriend, Detective Murphy went at once to Eleanor Temple's home on Herman Street and was surprised to discover that she had been dropped off only a few minutes after Robert Ross.

So what was Norman Bechtel doing parked behind an empty mansion around midnight? Had he gone to the Stokes estate alone? And who was the woman the trolley motorman heard screaming? Was it possible that the straight-laced church worker had picked up another woman after dropping off his girlfriend? The victim's aunt and uncle discounted this theory. "I don't believe it," said Joseph Bechtel. "Also, I've never heard of Norman having an enemy of any kind."

This opinion was shared by the victim's employer, Lloyd Schultz, who said that Norman was a hard worker and was well-liked by his colleagues. "He was a model young man, so far as I know," stated Schultz. "Morally he stood ace high. He came to work for us fourteen years ago and advanced rapidly."

Elsie Bechtel, Norman's forty-eight-year-old crippled step-sister, agreed with her uncle and Schultz. "He was sober and industrious," said Elsie. "He had no serious entanglements with any girl acquaintances and had no enemies." As for motive, Elsie believed that the murder was simply a case of mistaken identity. "I believe a gang of radicals thought Norman was Judge McDevitt," she said. "Norman was the same height as the judge and resembled him in many other respects." Detectives disagreed; Norman was a sturdy man of 180 pounds, while Judge McDevitt was slight of build. There could be little possibility of mistaking one for the other.

Lieutenant Frank Choplinski of the city homicide squad had his own theory. "How he got into that lonely section where his body was found is a mystery," he said to reporters. "I believe he was forced there. It looks as if they killed him in the car and dumped his body out."

Choplinski might not have been far off the mark; the following afternoon, Norman's car was found abandoned at the corner of Powelton and Thirty-second Streets in West Philadelphia, about five miles from the Stokes estate, and the automobile's interior was drenched in blood. A matted clump of hair was discovered on the driver's seat. Among the local residents questioned by police was the janitor of an apartment building who claimed that the car had been in the spot since four o'clock in the morning.

Norman's black coupe fit the description of the car that the trolley motorman had seen speeding along Westview Avenue, although Patrolman Lehman claimed to have seen a long sedan emerging from the Stokes driveway. This seemed to offer the possibility that Norman Bechtel had been attacked elsewhere and his dying body dumped on the

Detectives search Norman Bechtel's vehicle for clues. The tall figure is fingerprint expert Otis Shull. *Philadelphia Inquirer*, January 21, 1932.

grounds of Lone Oak. Norman's car was guarded by authorities until a fingerprint expert could arrive and examine it inch by inch. Much to their disappointment, fingerprint expert Otis Shull declared that the killer had worn gloves. Captain Harry Heanley of the homicide squad believed that Bechtel had been stabbed inside his car, which the killer then drove to the Stokes estate. It was here, he believed, the perpetrator had inflicted the other wounds after dragging Norman from the vehicle.

In the meantime, investigators worked on the theory that the murder could have been premeditated. Copies of Norman's will and life insurance policies were obtained from Lloyd Schultz and revealed that Norman's policies were valued at $22,000. This wasn't exactly chump change—in today's currency, it would equal nearly $250,000. But why would a healthy, unmarried, thirty-one-year-old man take out such a large policy? Captain Heanley was puzzled by this detail. "We would like to know why a bachelor of Bechtel's age would want to carry so much insurance," Heanley said to reporters. The beneficiaries were his step-sister, Elsie

Bechtel, and a brother, Wilbur, who resided in the Perkiomen Valley of Montgomery County. Incidentally, at the time of the murder, Wilbur was visiting Elsie at her home in Germantown. Norman had made out his will on December 4, 1929. Not surprisingly, Norman requested that all his possessions should go to Elsie and Wilbur.

TEMPLE QUESTIONED

With the time of the murder pinned down between the dropping off of Eleanor Temple at approximately 11:20 and the finding of the body at ten past midnight, authorities were confident in a quick resolution. They had already located Norman's car, and the headquarters of the homicide squad at City Hall had been bombarded with witnesses who were eager to tell detectives all they knew about the murdered church worker. On the night of January 21, they recited their stories before Captain Heanley's "war board" of investigators whose job it was to unravel the strange, and often contradictory, threads of Norman Bechtel's life. Those present included Assistant Superintendent of Police Joseph LeStrange and Assistant Director of Public Safety Theodore F. Wood. "Dory," as Assistant Director Wood was known, was no stranger to solving mysteries; he had been a detective for more than a quarter of a century and had previously served as Captain of the City Hall Detective Division.

One by one, the theories of detectives collapsed with each new revelation about the Mennonite church worker and witness accounts of what they had seen and heard the night of the murder. Detectives, however, were optimistic that the process of elimination would steer them in the direction of the killer or killers. They were especially eager to hear Eleanor Temple's version of events.

Eleanor, along with church superintendent Robert Ross, was questioned in detail between eight o'clock and 10:30, but neither could tell authorities anything they didn't already know about the events of January 19. Eleanor did disclose, however, that she had never been romantically involved with Norman. In fact, Eleanor said they weren't even very close friends. "My associations with Mr. Bechtel have extended only to church matters," insisted Eleanor. "I have never had a social engagement with him. His bringing me home last night was merely a matter of coincidence." According to Eleanor, she had purchased a train ticket to Lansdale as well as a return ticket but had nearly an hour to kill before taking the train back to Germantown. "Mr. Bechtel very kindly offered to drive me home. Of course, I accepted." Eleanor also stated that Norman had made no strange or telling remarks during the trip. "Coming down from Lansdale he seemed in good spirits, joking repeatedly. I didn't know him well enough to tell whether he might have had some secret trouble on his mind or not. Last night was the first time I had seen him for some time."

However, the interview produced a few possible avenues for further investigation; Norman always carried a small, open-faced ladies gold watch, which had once belonged to his mother. She had given him the watch as a boy, and ever since her death, he had carried it everywhere. This watch was not found on the victim's body or at the crime scene, though a piece of broken gold chain was found attached to Norman's lapel buttonhole. It was clear that the watch had been snatched violently from the victim's pocket, indicating a robbery motive. Police would turn their attention to local jewelry stores and pawn shops in case the missing watch showed up, while a jeweler with whom Norman had done business provided a detailed description of the timepiece. Temple and Ross also told police that Norman had a watch of his own, though they weren't sure if he was wearing it on the night of his death. A search of Norman's apartment failed to locate it, though police stumbled across his diary. It contained the names of several young men and women connected with his church and Boy Scout troop. But, as to anything else the diary may have contained, authorities refused to say.

After hearing from the witnesses, police investigators were left with only one inescapable conclusion: The killer must have been a man of unusual physical strength. Not only was the watch chain broken, but also the stab wounds on Bechtel's chest were exceptionally deep, even though the victim was wearing a heavy overcoat, a jacket, vest, dress shirt, and undershirt. The stiletto had even pierced a steel eyeglass case inside Norman's vest pocket. "The wounds were the thrusts of a powerful man," stated Dr. William Wadsworth, the physician who performed the post-mortem examination of the body.

The Black Bible and the All-Seeing Eye

While the stab wounds on the dead man's chest indicated a powerful thrust, the ritualistic carvings on Norman Bechtel's face, in contrast, suggested a delicate touch. Police described the markings as a crescent and a bar on each temple and three radiating lines high on the forehead: There was, on each temple, beginning at the top of the ear and pointing toward the nostril, a crescent-shaped wound, carved as if on wood—deliberate, careful, exact. On each cheekbone was a somewhat similar slash about two inches long. The press, understandably, was eager to learn more about these ritualistic wounds, as was the keeper of the Philadelphia Morgue. "These are the most peculiar wounds I ever saw in my years of varied experience," declared morgue superintendent William Condon. "The deliberate designs in which the wounds were cast resembles a sculptured, carved piece of work. I would certainly like to know the explanation."

Considering that Norman was born in raised in the Pennsylvania Dutch region of Berks County, many believed that the markings had something to do with hexerei or "pow-wow"—the Pennsylvania Dutch form of witchcraft.

The practice of braucherei (a form of white magic) and hexerei (a form of black magic) in Pennsylvania was known to outsiders since the early eighteenth century, when pow-wow "doctors" were hired by the afflicted to cast spells, cure illnesses, and ward off evil spirits. Some of these pow-wow doctors continued to operate well into the twentieth century, armed with strange rituals and incantations that have their roots in medieval Europe. Many Pennsylvania Dutch pow-wow doctors based their spells on writings found in The Six and Seventh Books of Moses, a magical text allegedly written by Moses and passed down as a "lost book" of the Hebrew Bible.

Though the origins of The Sixth and Seventh Books of Moses are shrouded in mystery, the oldest known copies were printed as pamphlets in Germany during the eighteenth century, and these pamphlets included instructions for performing such fantastical works as controlling the weather, exorcising demons, and communicating with the dead. These pamphlets also featured a variety of magical drawings and occult symbols. It is worth pointing out, however, that this mystical tome also influenced practitioners of other religions around the world, particularly Vodou and other magical practices in the Caribbean and West Africa. Between 1936 and 1972, folklorist Harry Middleton Hyatt conducted interviews with 1,600 African-American voodoo doctors and observed that many cited The Sixth and Seventh Books of Moses as a reference guide. This forbidden book of knowledge also found a home in Scandinavia and central Europe, where it was known as "The Black Bible."

While the figures carved on the victim's face do not tally with any of the symbols found within the Hebrew and Germanic versions of The Sixth and Seventh Books of Moses, the occult symbol, as described by police and the press, closely resembles the Eye of Providence, or the "all-seeing eye," as it is sometimes known. Some early Christian representations of the Eye of Providence depict three lines radiating from the eye, which are said to represent the Trinity. The all-seeing eye is also associated with Freemasonry, in which the symbol serves as a reminder that man's innermost thoughts and secret deeds are always observed by God.

But what sort of message had the killer been trying to convey by carving this symbol into Norman Bechtel's flesh? That he or she, like God, knew some deep, dark secret about the victim? Though Assistant Superintendent of Police Joseph LeStrange dismissed this idea, some reporters, along with many of the law enforcement officials who assisted in the investigation, believed this might have been the case. As for a possible connection with Pennsylvania Dutch witchcraft, Reverend Emanuel Cassel of a Mennonite church in Berks County had his doubts. "Mennonites are little concerned over what is said about them in this connection," said Reverend Cassel to the *Philadelphia Inquirer*. "Their faith in God and the tenets of religion are too sincere to permit them to believe in the occult or in 'pow-wow' arts."

Wilbur Bechtel, the victim's brother, also dismissed the witchcraft angle. "Up in the section in which we were raised nobody believes such things," he said. "Those practices occur further north. My brother used to laugh at the idea of people being cured of disease by pow-wowing and at the idea of casting spells. For years, if he needed medical treatment, he went to a physician."

A FAMILY CURSE?

In addition to the Philadelphia police, private investigators were also investigating the strange case of Norman Bechtel. One private investigator, Paul Kleinspehn, believed that the solution to the mystery might be obtained by examining the Bechtel family history, and he traveled to the region where Norman had been born. There, he learned of the uncanny fates of other members of the Bechtel clan (though it is debatable how closely related these families were related). In the fall of 1903, twenty-one-year-old Mabel Bechtel was found brutally murdered in the alleyway behind her mother's Allentown home. Her mother and brothers were accused of killing Mabel because she had rejected a suitor which her family believed would improve the family's financial condition and then tampering with the body in an attempt to pin the crime on a stranger. Her brother, Thomas, was arrested as the killer but committed suicide in jail. The other family members were tried as accessories after the fact but acquitted, leaving Mabel's murder, for all intents and purposes, unsolved.

Less than two years later, another Bechtel would fall victim to foul play. In February of 1905, the body of forty-five-year-old music teacher Harry K. Bechtel was found in a snowbank while on a business trip to Haddonfield, New Jersey. Harry, who lived in Pennsburg, seven miles from Norman Bechtel's childhood home, was robbed and stripped of his clothing before being beaten and left in a lonely spot to freeze to death. His killer was never caught. In a truly bizarre twist of fate, Harry's older brother, Dr. David Bechtel, burned to death in a Philadelphia hospital room in 1908. David, who was receiving treatment for a drug addiction, was burned to a crisp after it was determined that he reached from his bed to turn off a gaslight, which ignited the sleeve of his sleeping gown.

With these unfortunate happenings, it was only natural for some of the more superstitious residents of Germantown to claim that Norman Bechtel had been cursed from birth. Some even whispered that the killer might've been a Bechtel himself and had gouged out Norman's eyeball lest he, too, fall victim to the "evil eye." Detectives, on the other hand, paid little attention to these rumors. They had their hands full dealing with dark forces from the material world; let the mystics and witch doctors worry about the dark forces from the esoteric world. "I found nothing to give us a clue to these hex marks," said Captain Heanley. "Everything we found indicated he was an upright and honest young church worker. There was nothing to show that he belonged to any secret order."

First Suspect Arrested
The early consensus among investigators was that Norman Bechtel had been murdered by someone with whom he was acquainted, perhaps remotely, and of whom he was not suspicious. On January 21, Detective Murphy arrested a parking garage attendant named John Coles at his home on Norris Street. Having worked near Norman's apartment, Coles was familiar with the victim and his vehicle, and he became a person of interest after investigation revealed that Coles had left work early on the night of the murder. Coles was able to furnish an alibi, claiming that his boss had given him permission to leave at seven o'clock so that he could keep a date with his girlfriend near Reading. His story checked out, and he was released. Coles, incidentally, would again take center stage in the murder investigation five years later.

Funeral for a Fussy Man
The funeral services for Norman Bechtel were held at the Hereford Mennonite Church in Bally on the afternoon of January 24, but a preliminary service for Philadelphia friends and colleagues was held the night before at the funeral parlor of John K. Hackman on West Lehigh Avenue. It was reported that more than two thousand persons flocked to the funeral parlor to view the corpse, eager to catch a glimpse of the mysterious markings which the killer had delicately etched into Norman's face as he lay dying on a cold gravel driveway. They left disappointed—the morticians had done a skillful job hiding them from view.

Among those present at the evening service in Philadelphia were the two people who stood to gain the most from Norman's death, Elsie and Wilbur Bechtel. Also attending was a cousin from Philadelphia named Paul Clemer and several of Norman's work colleagues. All of these individuals had been interviewed by Captain Heanley earlier that evening and had promised to assist in the investigation. Yet nothing was learned by the time Norman's body was transported to Bally by automobile.

"Bechtel, apparently, was a somewhat taciturn individual," remarked Captain Heanley. "He was apparently a thinker and not a talker . . . he seldom revealed anything concerning himself." By this time, rumors of Norman's sexuality had been widely circulated, and the captain carefully addressed this topic of gossip. "From those we have examined we learned that he had few, if any, girlfriends and that he was a man who attempted to dress immaculately," continued Captain Heanley. "He was apparently a person of meticulous habits, perhaps even a trifle fussy." In the 1930s, this was about as close as one could come to saying that a man was homosexual without actually coming right out and saying it.

This revelation coincided with the victim's diary, which detectives had been hesitant to discuss. In his diary, Norman had made careful notations of his spending. While the Germantown accountant was stingy with most of his finances, he spared no expense on clothing, grooming, or personal comforts. His bank account showed a meager balance, and his spending on personal comforts seemed to have increased during the final years of his life. In a way, it was almost as if he were rebelling in secrecy against his upbringing among the "Plain People" of Berks County. This was also evidenced by a large number of stock certificates issued by "fly-by-night" corporations detectives found inside the apartment during a search on January 23. One newspaper article on the valuation of Norman's estate mentions "257 shares of stock in four companies appraised as having no value." Evidently, Norman was gambling that his questionable investments might someday make him an overnight millionaire—which leads one to wonder if the motive for his slaying might have had something to do with his flashy clothing and increasingly erratic spending. Perhaps somebody wanted to prevent Norman from throwing his money away while there was still time.

By all accounts, Norman's apartment was a testament to his "fussy" nature. Detectives were unable to find a speck of dust or a piece of furniture that was even the slightest bit crooked or disarranged. From the building's owner, Margaret Miller, investigators learned that Norman had no qualms about complaining about his apartment being too hot or too cold and had often chastised the chambermaid when she did not perform her work up to his demanding standards. The tenant's fussy temperament had even led to the firing of a janitor. According to Mrs. Miller, Norman would occasionally entertain "groups of men" inside his apartment, but she could not recall him ever entertaining a female visitor. Strangely, it seems that the world learned more about Norman Bechtel in death than was ever learned during his life. But while these details helped paint a picture of the private world of the Mennonite church worker, it did very little to move the investigation forward.

AN ABUNDANCE OF POSSIBILITIES, A SHORTAGE OF CLUES
While some investigators still held firm to the robbery motive, Captain Heanley, Assistant Superintendent LeStrange, and Assistant Director of Public Safety Dory Wood found the details a bit too peculiar for such a simple explanation. Why would a robber go through the trouble of adding additional stab wounds around the heart after inflicting the one that was most certainly fatal? Why take the victim's wallet but leave the seventeen dollars? Why steal the car only to abandon it a short time later? It was increasingly beginning to look like a staged robbery, and this left the detectives wondering if the deliberately etched symbols had been staged as well. If such was the case, this might suggest that the killer was someone who had gone through great lengths to conceal his or her true motive. But what could that motive be?

One detail which seemed to defy explanation was the placement of the body. Assuming that Norman had been stabbed soon after dropping Eleanor Temple off at her home by an unidentified assailant inside his own vehicle, which bloodstains clearly indicated, why would the killer transport Norman in his own car to Lone Oak? If Patrolman Lehman had been correct when he said that he saw "a long sedan" pulling out of the driveway and not Norman's smaller and sportier coupe, it stood to reason that multiple persons were involved in the crime. It was almost as if someone else had been waiting at Lone Oak for the body to arrive. Assuming this theory is correct, it might also be possible that the fatal heart wound and the ritualistic carvings were made by two different hands.

The "war board" of the city's top investigators mulled over these points, and everything pointed back to Lone Oak. The estate of Thomas

P. C. Stokes became the object of renewed interest, and the detectives and officers who had scoured the grounds earlier for a murder weapon were instructed to conduct an inch-by-inch search inside the home and garage. Unfortunately, during the brief period when authorities had relaxed their vigilance, curiosity seekers had besieged the grounds and vandalized the property. The trunk of the cherry tree under which Bechtel's body was found had been whittled almost to the point of destruction by souvenir hunters armed with pocketknives, and police doubted that it could be saved. The only moment of excitement occurred during the search of the garage when a stained chauffeur's cap was found. Believing that the dark stains might be blood, the cap was sent off for analysis. The stains proved to be oil.

Police also timed the drive from Temple's apartment to the Stokes estate and determined that it would have taken approximately eight minutes. By their best estimates, the coupe seen by the trolley motorman sped away from the death scene fifteen minutes after Temple had been dropped off. So where had Norman Bechtel spent those missing seven minutes?

By Monday, January 25, thirty-four detectives had been working on the murder investigation full-time and 115 individuals had been questioned. These included relatives, co-workers, neighbors, church members, and even childhood acquaintances from Berks County. Not even the pastor who officiated Norman's funeral in Bally was spared a visit from detectives, nor the eighteen members of the Young Peoples' Retreat Committee. Some detectives had been roused from their beds to tail persons of interest in the middle of the night, and others had been sent on wild goose chases in remote regions, but none had succeeded in finding evidence.

Leads, on the other hand, were plentiful, and police vowed to explore each and every one until the case was solved. "The investigation must necessarily be one of elimination," stated Assistant Director Wood. "We are seeking to check every possible theory, and then, as each is proven unfeasible, move on to the next." These leads included an anonymous letter mailed to the undertaker who prepared Norman's body in which the writer had claimed that the victim was having an affair with a friend's wife, and a key case found among the leaves on the grounds of Lone Oak. These leads, like the others, proved to be as fruitless as Thomas Stokes' cherry tree.

BROTHER OFFERS REWARD

On January 26, a reward of one thousand dollars was teased by Wilbur Bechtel for information leading to the arrest of his brother's killer. "This reward would not be offered as an incentive for further detective investigation," explained Wilbur. "I have the greatest confidence in the local police department and I'm sure the men are doing all they can to solve the mystery. However, I am of the opinion that there may be someone possessing information that would help the detectives, and he will be induced by the reward to tell what he knows."

After consulting with his brother's attorney, Maxwell Kratz, and the Philadelphia police, Wilbur finally posted the reward on February 3, stating that the reward money would come from his brother's estate. Incidentally, this was the same day Norman's estate was adjudicated in court. With the exception of $1,500 that Norman had bequeathed to two Mennonite churches, the entire estate, which was valued at $25,148, was inherited by Elsie and Wilbur Bechtel. No relatives contested the will.

Five hundred posters announcing the reward were distributed throughout Germantown and surrounding neighborhoods, while additional posters were distributed throughout the Perkiomen Valley. Strangely, all of the posters tacked on poles in the vicinity of the murder were mysteriously torn down within the following three days. Acting on the assumption that the party responsible for the murder was ripping down the posters, a number of plainclothes officers were swiftly dispatched to Germantown to keep watch. Yet, under their very noses, the remaining posters came down, one by one. The posters were replaced on February 9, only to be ripped down again the next day. While some detectives attributed this action to souvenir-seekers, this doesn't explain why the undercover policemen were unable to catch any of the culprits in the act. Wilbur Bechtel would later retract the reward.

SHERLOCK HOLMES WEIGHS IN

On February 9, Detective Murphy and Lieutenant Choplinski traveled to the Montgomery County jail in Norristown to question inmates who answered the description of two black men who were seen near Norman Bechtel's abandoned coupe shortly after the murder. The two men, who had been picked up after a store robbery on January 25, were identified as James Crawford and Rudy Harrison of Philadelphia. At the time, Crawford was carrying a long, thin knife. Experts examined the knife and agreed that it would have been able to inflict Norman's wounds. The inmates were kept in solitary confinement but were eventually exonerated in the Bechtel case.

By this time, "The Mennonite Mystery," as some called it, was attracting attention throughout the country, and some of the biggest names in law enforcement weighed in on the case. One such expert was Ellis H. Parker, chief of Burlington County detectives in New Jersey. His dapper mustache, bowler hat, and pipe not withstanding, Parker was widely considered one of the top detectives in America, and perhaps one of the earliest proponents of psychological profiling in the Unites States. It was Parker who would solve the case of the kidnapping of the Lindbergh baby a few years later, earning him the nickname "The American Sherlock Holmes" (although the pipe probably helped).

Parker believed that nothing short of a miracle would result in the capture of the Evil Eye Killer. "I would say the murder looks like the work of a mental deficient," said Parker. "That makes it an exceedingly difficult task. I would say there is little chance to solve the case except through accident or a lucky chance." Detective Parker based this opinion on a lack of a motive, and Parker, like most top detectives (real or fictional), believed that motive is everything. "Nothing has been disclosed to furnish a clue," he continued. "This tends to strengthen the probability that the killer of Bechtel had no grudge against him and was moved only by the impulses of an unsound mind. The illogical ferocity with which Bechtel was stabbed and slashed also seems to confirm this."

THE MYSTERIOUS SCREAM

Patrolman Lehman, the trolley motorman, and another nearby police-man all reported hearing the wild scream of a woman as the killer sped away in the victim's car, and countless hours were devoted to solving the mystery of this chilling shriek. It was this high-pitched feminine scream, paired with the lack of a female body, which initially led Detective Murphy to believe that Eleanor Temple had been kidnapped by Norman Bechtel's murderer. But Assistant Superintendent Joseph LeStrange asked himself, "What if the scream had come from Bechtel himself?" Up to this point, none of the detectives had thought to ask witnesses about the victim's voice, but LeStrange remembered Eleanor's claim that Norman was cracking jokes on the ride back from Lansdale. He wondered if Norman's voice reached a higher pitch when frightened or excited, and his questioning of Norman's closest friends confirmed his suspicion. On February 10, LeStrange issued a statement stating that it was his belief that the "female scream" heard on the night of the murder was the sound of the victim in mortal agony—perhaps the agony of one's eye being torn from its socket.

Meanwhile, a closer examination of the bloody driver's seat of Norman's automobile strengthened Captain Heanley's belief that the victim received the fatal chest wound while sitting behind the wheel. The cushion of the seat was bloody, but most of the blood spilled onto the left side of the cushion, running down the edge and pooling against the driver's side door. Blood could not have dripped from the clothes of the murderer in such a manner.

On February 12, hopes were raised with the finding of a box of books in the basement of the Paramount Court Apartments on West Venango Street. The box, which contained textbooks and papers from Norman's time in college, provided detectives with the names of classmates and instructors who had yet to be questioned. Ultimately, none were able to furnish any new information. With a lack of motive and scant evidence, a shortage of leads and an exhausted army of detectives, authorities pinned their dwindling hopes on the coroner's inquest, which was to be held the following week.

An Indifferent Inquest

On Thursday, February 18, the citizens of Philadelphia waited with bated breath to hear what startling revelations would emerge from Coroner Fred Schwarz's inquest, which would be the first official hearing in the murder case. The coroner had announced that the public was excluded from attending and that a special detail of police would be placed around the building to discourage interference from the overly curious.

"There is no use wasting time over this," Coroner Schwarz said to reporters clamoring for a preview. "We are not going to spend hours when there is not any testimony that means anything, and we are not going to put on a circus for the benefit of morbid, curious people."

While over one hundred persons had been quizzed by detectives, the testimony was limited to only six witnesses, with the testimony of Dr. William Wadsworth being the most anticipated. Wadsworth, the coroner's physician, was noted for his painstaking autopsies, which, in the past, had yielded clues overlooked by the city homicide squad. Wadsworth was also known for his refusal to divulge any of his findings until he had a chance to give testimony before the coroner's jury. Other witnesses who were listed to testify included Lieutenant Detective Choplinski, Patrolman Lehman, and Detective Bernard O'Donnell. An uncle, Aaron Bechtel (who shared a home with Elsie), was also called to testify, as was a cousin, Paul Clemer of Shelmire Street. Wilbur Bechtel, Eleanor Temple, and Robert Ross attended as spectators but were not asked to testify.

Assistant District Attorney Norris S. Barratt asked Dr. Wadsworth only five questions, in what was probably the shortest testimony he had ever given during an inquest. "You performed a postmortem on the body of Norman R. Bechtel?" asked Barratt.

"Yes," replied Dr. Wadsworth.

"What was the cause of death?"

"Stab wounds."

"More than one?"

"A number," answered Dr. Wadsworth.

"Could you tell which one caused death?"

"Several contributed."

Patrolman Lehman was asked to recite what he had seen and heard the night he found the body and nothing more. Choplinski and O'Donnell were the next witnesses called. When asked by the coroner if they had anything to add to Lehman's testimony, both replied: "Nothing further."

The only other question asked was by James McLea, the attorney representing Wilbur Bechtel, who wanted to establish whether or not Norman Bechtel came by his wounds inside his automobile. The reason for this question, evidently, was purely financial: Norman's life insurance policy contained a double indemnity clause, in which the value of the payout would be doubled if Norman had died from injuries sustained inside his car.

In total, the purely perfunctory proceedings lasted a mere twenty minutes, revealing precious little except for the financial interests of the beneficiaries; seven months later, Wilbur Bechtel would file suit in the Court of Common Pleas against the Continental Casualty Company to recover double indemnity on his brother's policy, arguing that the fatal wound had been inflicted while Norman was inside the vehicle.

A SECRET SOCIETY SERIAL KILLER?

The hasty inquest, not surprisingly, did little to squelch the rumors and gossip surrounding the case. After the strange death of Lansdale foundry night watchman Samuel Forti on February 18, many believed that both crimes had been carried out by the same killer. This was based on one Montgomery County police chief's claims that Forti, a forty-five-year-old father of ten, was a member of a secret society.

Forti's trussed body was found suspended from a plank across two lockers in the washroom of the Werner Foundry. Strips of rags, cut from the lining of a man's coat, were used to tie his hands behind his back, while a leather belt had been used to bind the feet. Forti had been struck viciously in the face and body while in the throes of strangulation. According to Lansdale Chief of Police Samuel Woffindin, the dead watchman belonged to a religious cult, and he believed that Forti was murdered because he wanted out. Chief Woffindin based his opinion on the fact that a Bible, written in Italian, was missing from Forti's work

Wilbur Bechtel (left) with Lieutenant Choplinski at the coroner's inquest. *Philadelphia Inquirer*, February 18, 1932.

locker. Woffindin (who, incidentally, was an acquaintance of Norman Bechtel) believed that the inner secrets of the cult, and the names of its members, were contained in the stolen Bible.

Like Norman, the night watchman from Lansdale had no known enemies, but it seemed clear that somebody, for some reason, wanted him dead. Harry Long, the foundry foreman who found the body, told police that Forti had appeared extremely nervous in the days leading up to his death; he was afraid to step outside after dark (not exactly a good trait for a night watchman) and chose to spend his lunch breaks alone in the locker room reading his Bible. Forti had been eating a sandwich when he was struck over the head with a blunt instrument, then bound hand and foot and hanged from the improvised gallows. Nothing, except for the contents of Forti's locker, appeared to have been disturbed or stolen.

Because of its religious connotations and the fact that Forti's murder occurred a little over one month later, in the same town from which Norman had departed on the night of his death, Chief Woffindin believed that the murders were carried out by the same person. He also believed the murderer had tailed Norman's vehicle from the church meeting in Lansdale, waiting until Bechtel was alone in the car before stabbing him through the heart. Chief Woffindin shared his theory with Captain Heanley, who assigned a handful of his best detectives to work with the Lansdale police, but they were unable to connect the two murders.

While the murder of Samuel Forti also remains unsolved, it is doubtful (though certainly not impossible) that the two slayings were carried out by the same person. One victim was mutilated, the other bludgeoned and hanged. Though Forti's involvement in a "secret society" was later confirmed, the group in question was comprised solely of Italian Catholics who called themselves Chiesa Christiana Delle Fede Apostalica, or "Church of Christ of Faith in Apostles," and it was later revealed that Forti had been having an affair with the sect's founder, a Philadelphia woman named Julia Sesantis. Norman, on the other hand, was neither Italian nor Catholic, had no interest in women, and he was quite happy with the Mennonite church. Although the State Police investigation concluded that Forti's death was a suicide (doubtful, as self-hanging victims tend not to bludgeon themselves and tie up their hands and feet),

Woffindin insisted that it had been murder and vowed to continue the investigation alone, to no avail. On a strange sidenote, the missing Bible around which the Forti investigation was centered was later found inside Forti's home. How it got there remains a mystery.

SUGARFOOT GREEN AND THE END OF LONE OAK

With elderly Ellen Welsh Stokes getting her affairs in order and making her final arrangements from her residence in Delaware County, the residents of Germantown wondered what would become of the Lone Oak estate. A clue was offered in early August, when workmen began removing furniture from the unoccupied house. It was Mrs. Stokes' wish to have the furniture donated to the needy. On August 16, a crew from the Central House Wrecking Company arrived to demolish the home, bringing an end to the Lone Oak estate and the loss of whatever undiscovered evidence that may have been left behind on that fateful night in January.

After the strange death of Samuel Forti in Lansdale, the Bechtel investigation ground to a halt. Philadelphia's best detectives were stumped, but until a new break came in the case, their efforts were needed elsewhere in the city. On December 5, Captain Heanley identified a new person of interest and handed one of his top investigators, Detective Michael C. Croskey, an undercover assignment. For Croskey, it would prove to be his final assignment.

Three teenage boys, bundled against the winter chill, were walking along Powelton Avenue on the rainy evening of December 7. It was shortly after five o'clock, but the city was steeped in darkness as the boys rounded the corner onto Sloan Street, just in time to hear the rumbling of an engine and see a car pulling into a garage. It was Detective Croskey, returning home from a second day of working on the Bechtel case. One of the boys, fifteen-year-old Joseph Graham, saw a man place his hand on the detective's shoulder. "Well, Mike, I've got you now, and you're not going to get away," he heard the man say. The teenagers recognized the man as George "Sugarfoot" Green, the driver of a neighborhood ice truck. Words were exchanged inside the garage when, suddenly, the detective made a strange gurgling noise. As Sugarfoot Green fled on foot into the night, Detective Croskey staggered out of the garage and fell onto the sidewalk.

Croskey's mother and brother were a few feet away inside the home when they heard Michael's car pulling into the garage. Minutes passed, but the thirty-eight-year-old never entered the house. Growing concerned, the detective's mother went outside, just in time to see her son being placed into an unfamiliar automobile by a woman she did not recognize. This would be a concerned passerby flagged down for assistance by the three teenagers. She sped away from the curb and drove the wounded detective to Presbyterian Hospital, where he died from his injuries. Five stab wounds to the neck by an ice pick had severed Croskey's jugular vein.

The possibility of a link between the deaths of Detective Croskey and Norman Bechtel was cause for excitement. Just hours before his death, the detective had told close friends that he had "something pretty good to look into" concerning the Bechtel murder. Before the blood inside the garage had a chance to dry, the scene was swarming with law enforcement; Inspector Earl LaReau, Detective Lieutenant Perry Jeffers, Patrolman Michael Hardiman, and Assistant Director of Public Safety Dory Wood were at the Croskey home within minutes.

As for the detective's killer, the ice truck driver was well-known to authorities. Described by the *Philadelphia Inquirer* as a "Negro bad man" and a "cop-hater" with a lengthy rap sheet, Sugarfoot Green had pummeled one officer in 1916 before firing a bullet at the head of another. He fired shots at two other officers in 1921, and while being placed under arrest in 1925, Green attempted to stab the arresting officer with an ice pick. Green was a strong man with a sharp, thin object—exactly the type of suspect authorities had been seeking in the Bechtel case—and the fact that he had ambushed Croskey as the detective was homing in on the most promising lead to date seemed to suggest a connection. But, if such a connection did exist, it was never found. Green was eventually sentenced to six to twelve years for involuntary manslaughter after claiming that his attack on Croskey was in self-defense.

It will probably never be known just what, if anything, Croskey managed to find out during his brief foray into the Bechtel case. Not just because of his untimely demise, but also because the foundations of City Hall were about to be rocked by one of the biggest shake-ups in the history of the Philadelphia Police Department.

CAPTAIN BUYS KEY PIECE OF EVIDENCE

While Detective Croskey lay dying in a pool of blood, city council was voting on a measure that would greatly handicap the police force. As a cost-cutting measure, city council slashed from the payroll five hundred patrolmen, 120 detectives, fifty street sergeants, seventeen desk sergeants, eighteen police captains, and thirteen inspectors. On December 10, it was leaked that Superintendent of Police William B. Mills was preparing to tender his resignation to accept the position as new warden of Holmesburg Prison, thereby putting the jobs of Public Safety Director Kern Dodge, Assistant Superintendent Joseph LeStrange, and Assistant Director Dory Wood in jeopardy. In other words, just about every person whose fingerprints were on the Bechtel casefiles had either been purged from the force or was at risk of demotion or reassignment whenever the mayor appointed a new superintendent.

Director Dodge's days had appeared numbered ever since an explosive city council meeting the previous week, in which Councilman Harry Trainer accused the public safety director of conspiring with underworld racketeers and demanded that Dodge "show his manhood" by resigning. Captain of Detectives Harry Heanley was also facing demotion after becoming the target of an internal investigation ordered by Director Dodge, charging the captain with "general inefficiency" and dereliction of duty for failing to solve a number of murder cases, including the Bechtel case. In his complaint against Heanley, Director Dodge accused the captain of violating regulations by purchasing a key piece of evidence—the car in which Norman Bechtel had been stabbed. The captain, who purchased the coupe from Wilbur Bechtel, had failed to fill out the appropriate forms and paperwork from the chief clerk of the police bureau.

The purchasing of the death car puzzled Director Dodge and other city officials, as the murder investigation was still open. They had heard of corrupt law enforcement officials destroying and tampering with evidence, but never had they heard of anyone buying evidence from an ongoing investigation. What would happen to the vehicle if Norman's killer was caught? Presumably, Captain Heanley had convinced himself that the mystery would never be solved and that the death car would never be needed as evidence, as he had already reupholstered the seats and had given the interior a thorough cleaning.

Aside from Captain Heanley's mishandling of evidence, Director Dodge's internal investigation uncovered gross mismanagement of several other murder cases. In 1932, Heanley's homicide squad solved just twenty of its 144 homicide cases. Fugitives no longer felt the need to flee the city because they were able to walk the streets without fear of capture. Dodge also discovered that Heanley and his detectives failed to arrest doctors accused of performing illegal abortions and intimated that the abortionists had escaped prosecution by paying off detectives.

When the dust settled, Assistant Superintendent Joseph LeStrange was appointed acting superintendent (his predecessor having taken the Holmesburg warden job), while Harry Heanley was demoted. However, there is an appalling sidenote attached to the resignation of William B. Mills; as warden of Holmesburg Prison, Mills was at the helm during the infamous "Bake-Oven" torture scandal of 1938, when four inmates were roasted to death by 200-degree steam after being placed into an isolation cell for protesting living conditions inside the facility. Warden Mills, along with nine other prison officials, were arrested and charged with manslaughter in the deaths of the four inmates. Governor Earle, after inspecting the prison, described Mills and his co-defendants as "the cruelest sadists who ever lived." When the fates of the defendants were put before a jury on June 23, 1939, all but two were acquitted. While Mills escaped justice for his role in the inhumane torture, his reputation was tarnished beyond repair, and he would never hold another position in law enforcement.

The shake-up within the police department also extended to the mayor's office and may have possibly played a role in Mayor Moore's decision not to seek re-election. The murder of Norman Bechtel occurred just days after J. Hampton Moore took office in 1932, and the homicide squad's failure to catch the Evil Eye Killer was a source of embarrassment to the man who had been swept into office on a promise to stamp out corruption and clean up the streets of Philadelphia. Moore, a Republican, won the 1931 mayoral election with a 92 percent majority, but the scandals within the police department led to widespread distrust of city officials. In 1935, Samuel Davis Wilson, also a Republican, won the 1935 mayoral election with just 53 percent of the vote, nearly bringing an end to the monopoly which the Republican Party had held in Philadelphia since 1884 (between 1884 and 1952, sixteen of the city's seventeen mayors were Republican, while one was an independent who ran on a campaign of reform). Since 1952, no Republican has been mayor of the city.

A CHAUFFEUR'S CONFESSION: BECHTEL KILLED BY A DEAD MAN

On the morning of April 15, 1937, Philadelphia awoke to a sensational announcement. Mayor Wilson, with his usual bombastic aplomb, declared from the Twenty-eighth and Oxford Streets police station that the Norman Bechtel mystery was finally solved after five years, on the strength of a confession given by a thirty-six-year-old chauffeur named William Jordan. Five persons, all of whom were black, were said to have participated in the crime, and the chauffeur had been in police custody since his arrest five days earlier.

As for the motive, Mayor Wilson refused to discuss it with the press. "It is very complicated," he said. "I cannot explain it at this moment. It might be a combination of a grudge over the loss of a job . . . plus an unpleasant angle I don't even want to discuss." Wilson added that Jordan had never been questioned by police during the original investigation, even though Jordan knew Norman personally. But the most curious part of Jordan's confession was that the man who actually stabbed the Mennonite church worker had died years earlier. So what had compelled this accomplice to come clean five years after the murder?

"Almost the moment my investigators questioned him, he began to give the information we wanted," said the mayor. "He said he had lost thirty pounds worrying over the killing and was glad to get it off his mind. He says he feels better now." Jordan's criminal record, however, does not reflect the image of a man compelled by guilt to spill the beans; the chauffeur had seven prior arrests, including an arrest for a hit-and-run that left the victim dead. Jordan was tried on manslaughter charges but acquitted.

It was Captain John Murphy who secured the chauffeur's confession. According to Jordan's statement, he had seen Norman stabbed eight times with a short knife as he sat behind the wheel of his car. The killer then climbed into the vehicle. With Norman still slumped over the wheel, the killer drove the car to the Stokes estate in Germantown. There, he dragged the semi-conscious victim to the spot under the cherry tree and stabbed him several more times with the same knife.

This confession, of course, is problematic; no fingerprints were found on either the steering wheel or the door handles, and physicians who examined Norman, along with Captain Heanley, were certain that only the fatal chest wound had been inflicted while the victim was inside the automobile. Physicians also described twenty stab wounds, of which only eight were in the chest, and these eight wounds formed a perfect circle. This hardly seems possible from a killer thrusting a knife through a car window in the dead of night. Also, Jordan described the weapon as a short knife, whereas physicians and detectives agreed that the fatal chest could only have been inflicted with a long, thin knife. Furthermore, the undertaker who prepared the body was convinced that the mysterious markings on Norman's face had been inflicted by a different weapon, and the dozens of detectives and police officers who examined the victim's body agreed on this point. And, finally, it seems highly improbable that the killer would be able to drive the car with Norman slumped over the wheel all the way to Lone Oak. Assuming that Norman was stabbed immediately after dropping Eleanor Temple off at her home at 129 Herman Street, this means the killer had to steer from the passenger seat a distance of more than twenty city blocks to the Stokes estate—a circuitous route with numerous left- and right-hand turns. How did he brake and accelerate? How did he reach the clutch? If one were to assume that the killer had squeezed himself into the driver's seat, this would not account for the pooling of blood in the space between the left edge of the seat and door, while the lack of blood on the passenger seat proves that Norman hadn't been placed there during the drive to Lone Oak.

THE FIRST NATIONAL BANK OF WILBUR

Despite these glaring inaccuracies, the boastful mayor was quick to give himself a pat on the back. "At present, I wish to say only this: that this was one of the crimes that I swore to solve when I became mayor," he stated. "From the day I took office I assigned the job of re-checking on the crime to Detectives Warren Murphy, Joseph Boston, and Francis O'Connell. Since that time, they have worked literally day and night." Mayor Wilson was also quick to point out the unethical behavior of detectives during the term of his predecessor, Mayor J. Hampton Moore, citing the fact that Wilbur Bechtel had not only sold his brother's bloody automobile to Captain Heanley, but he had also loaned $2,800 to Detective Choplinski.

"And I learned that he never paid it back!" added Mayor Wilson. "For that I reduced him to a patrolman."

It was also reported that Mayor Wilson had learned, upon taking office, that many important papers pertaining to the investigation had been lost or destroyed, including Norman Bechtel's diary.

Later that evening, Mayor Wilson called Wilbur Bechtel and the victim's cousin, Paul Clemer, to his office in city hall. There were a few things the mayor wanted cleared up, including Wilbur's reasons for telling the press that the chauffeur's confession was phony. "I don't believe the confession," Wilbur had told reporters earlier. "During the last five years I have spent a lot of money on many false clues, and I have no faith in the new development." Under the mayor's grilling, however, Wilbur recanted his statement and declared that he was satisfied that Jordan's confession was legitimate. Mayor Wilson then asked about the reward.

"Why did you offer a reward of $1,000 for solution of the crime and then, after a year, withdraw it?" demanded the mayor.

"That was necessary so the estate could be settled," answered Wilbur. "I always wanted a solution." The mayor then drilled the victim's brother about the loans he had made to Detective Choplinski and the selling of Norman's coupe to Captain Heanley.

"What did he want the money for?" the mayor asked.

"He said he owed money on a house and would lose it if he didn't pay up," replied Wilbur. He explained that he later made a second loan to

Choplinski for $800 because the detective had told him that his brother "was in trouble." When the mayor asked if he had ever loaned money to a stranger before, Wilbur said that he had not. Next, the mayor quizzed him about the sale of the automobile to Captain Heanley, for which Wilbur received $250.

"Didn't you know you were selling evidence?" roared Mayor Wilson. Wilbur innocently replied that he hadn't regarded the sale in that light. When quizzed about Norman's missing diary, Wilbur admitted that he was aware it had disappeared but said that he was out of town at the time.

Selling evidence, stealing evidence, misplacing evidence, borrowing money from a witness—it almost seems like a conspiracy or, at the very least, a quid pro quo between detectives and the man who was the primary beneficiary of a murder victim's life insurance policy. It was almost as if someone had said, "Now that you're about to come into some big money, we can make your brother's diary and its detailed entries about his sexual perversions disappear—for a price." Or perhaps detectives had agreed, for a cut of the insurance payout, to make it appear as if Norman Bechtel had been behind the wheel of the car in order to allow Wilbur to cash in on the policy's double-indemnity clause. With so much corruption running rampant within the police department, anything was possible, and Mayor Wilson vowed to get to the bottom of it.

Speakeasies and Silk Underwear

At noon on April 15, a few hours before Mayor Wilson's meeting with Wilbur Bechtel and Paul Clemer, William Jordan was brought to the mayor's reception room and confronted with the three friends he had implicated in the murder. These were thirty-year-old Fletcher Williams, twenty-nine-year-old Lucille Scott Young, and the very first man arrested in connection with the slaying—former garage attendant John Coles. According to Jordan, it was Coles who lured Norman to his rendezvous with death.

Jordan's friends listened with blank expressions as the chauffeur explained that he, Williams, and Coles, along with the actual killer, a janitor named Oliver Armstrong, had spent the night drinking at a speakeasy operated by Lucille Young, with Armstrong footing the bill. When

Armstrong's cash began to run out, Coles went to the garage where he worked and attempted to borrow money, to no avail. When he returned to the speakeasy, they resumed drinking until late in the evening. At this point, Coles suggested they hop into his car and accompany him to the corner of Westview Street and Wissahickon Avenue, where Coles had already planned to meet Norman. When Coles saw Norman's black coupe approaching, he got out of his car and signaled for the Mennonite church worker to stop.

According to Jordan, who remained inside the parked vehicle, Oliver Armstrong got out when Norman's car came to a stop. "Armstrong got on the running board on the driver's side of the car," stated Jordan. "He started an argument with Bechtel. They were talking very fast and I couldn't make out what they were saying, but the argument lasted four or five minutes. Then Armstrong started striking Bechtel with his head." At this, Mayor Wilson interrupted.

"Did you see the knife carried by Armstrong?" he asked.

"Yes, I did," replied Jordan. "It was a small penknife. Armstrong struck at him through the open window, then Bechtel slumped down in the car. Armstrong wanted John Coles to drive Bechtel's car, but Coles said he couldn't, so Armstrong got in the car and Coles came back to our car and got in." Jordan claimed that Armstrong then pulled Norman out of his car and dragged him under the cherry tree before getting back into Norman's coupe and ordering his friends to follow him. "But he was going at such a reckless speed that we lost sight of him, though we knew where he was going," Jordan continued. They followed Armstrong to a garage, and Armstrong got back into their sedan, and they drove to another speakeasy for another round of drinks.

This explanation corroborates the accounts of witnesses who saw both a coupe and a long sedan in the vicinity of the Stokes estate, but it fails to explain how a tiny penknife could penetrate Norman's steel spectacle case, winter overcoat, suit jacket, vest, dress shirt, and breastbone. Jordan also failed to make mention of the strange symbols carved into Norman's face or the stolen watches. And what about the motive? This thought occurred to Mayor Wilson as the four suspects were being led away. He called them back.

"Wait! Do you know of any reason why Armstrong would have trouble with Bechtel?" he asked.

"I think it was a disagreement because of the loss of Armstrong's job," replied Jordan. "He was the janitor at Bechtel's apartment and he said that Bechtel caused him to be fired."

"Where is Armstrong now?" asked the mayor.

"Armstrong died about two years ago. He went to sleep and never woke up again."

"How did you know that Bechtel would be at the corner of Wissahickon Avenue and Westview Street that night?" asked the mayor. Jordan claimed not to know. At this point, the mayor turned to Detective Warren Murphy and Captain John Murphy. Jordan's story was not the same version he had given during his confession, the version which had Armstrong getting into Norman's car—with the victim dying at the wheel—and driving it to Lone Oak. The mayor also found it strange that none of the other suspects had spoken a word; it was as if someone had appointed Jordan to do all the talking. But, whether the four suspects knew it or not, Mayor Wilson had read excerpts transcribed from the dead man's diary before its mysterious disappearance, and he was about to let the cat out of the bag. He motioned for John Coles to step forward.

"Did Norman Bechtel ever buy you silk underwear?" asked the mayor, followed by a barrage of highly personal questions.

"No, sir, Bechtel never bought me any silk underwear," Coles answered. "I had no date with Bechtel that night."

Fletcher Williams and Lucille Scott Young were asked if they had anything to say, and both denied being near the Stokes estate the night of the murder. Young was particularly indignant. "If I know anything about this case, why wait until now to lock me up?" she protested. "I've never been out with these men in any old car in my life! I've never run no speakeasy. It's a shame to take somebody in cold blood and accuse them of murder. Why should I be held without bail for something I know nothing about? And there's my little fifteen-year-old girl at home with no money."

"She'll get along," replied Mayor Wilson, adding that he had been able to fend for himself just fine at the same age. It was obvious that the mayor was unswayed by Young's outburst; he had already looked into her criminal record and got her to admit that she had been previously arrested on charges of tussling with a man over a gun, liquor law violations, and gambling. She admitted that police had searched her home at that time but found no gambling receipts—what the police claimed was evidence of numbers slips had been "dream books," as Lucille was heavily interested in numerology and astrology.

Attempted Suicide

While the suspects waited for the grand jury, they were held in a jail cell at the 40th District Station. On April 20, William Jordan attempted to slash his throat with a razor blade, resulting in six stitches. Mayor Wilson instructed Captain John Murphy to question every police officer at the station to determine how Jordan had obtained the dangerous contraband. Captain Murphy also found a second razor blade stitched between the layers of Jordan's coat collar. Jordan refused to answer any questions about the blade. The four inmates were then transferred to Moyamensing Prison, where they could be watched more closely by guards. The attempted suicide led Mayor Wilson to believe that Jordan knew more about the murder than he had admitted, as his story kept changing, while detectives pondered if Jordan might've been the real killer all along. "Whether, as one of the principals, Jordan hoped to save himself from the electric chair, or whether, as he said, his conscience troubled him and he wanted to relieve his mind, I don't know," said the mayor. "He might also have been seeking revenge on someone. His attempted suicide further complicates the situation."

Indictment

On April 28, the grand jury returned indictments against the four suspects. Meanwhile, Captain John Murphy and Detective Warren Murphy were in Lawrence, Massachusetts, interviewing a witness who claimed to have seen a car leaving the Stokes estate on the night of Norman's murder. The witness, a man by the name of Morgan, identified Lucille Scott Young as the woman he had seen driving an automobile from a photograph produced by Captain Murphy. "I am certain she is the woman I saw," stated Morgan. "I had a good view of her when the car she was driving stopped near a street light, and I noticed a deep scar over the bridge of her nose." Morgan, who had been living in Philadelphia at the time, encountered the vehicle along Wissahickon Avenue, and he vividly recalled the incident because the woman's erratic driving had nearly caused him to crash.

Morgan told Captain Murphy that Young was alone in the car but that it was followed by another automobile in which were "several Negroes." While this new piece of information contradicted Jordan's confession, it does corroborate the statement made by the trolley motorman who claimed to have seen Norman Bechtel's black coupe speeding down Wissahickon Avenue. Is it possible that Lucille Scott Young was the one who carved the mysterious occult symbols into Norman's face after Oliver Armstrong had delivered the fatal stab? This seems possible, considering Young's fascination with astrology.

BEATEN SENSELESS BY DETECTIVES

On May 19, 1937, William Jordan went on trial before Judge Albert Millar, who had decided to try the defendants separately. Prior to the trial, District Attorney Charles C. Gordon told reporters that he would not seek the death penalty for Jordan but that he intended to establish "undue intimacy" between Norman Bechtel and John Coles and to prove that this is what had led the four defendants to lure the victim to the Stokes estate. During the trial, Jordan reiterated his claims that he and his three friends had not actively participated in the murder—they had merely been in the wrong place at the wrong time. It was Oliver Armstrong who murdered Norman, insisted Jordan. Alexander Perry, defense attorney for William Jordan, claimed that his client's confession had been obtained by force and that he had been "plied with beer" to make him talk more readily.

On the witness stand, Jordan testified that he had been beaten repeatedly by detectives, who allegedly forced him to memorize the details of the case prior to his city hall meeting with Mayor Wilson. "I was arrested on Saturday, April 10, and between 2:00 p.m. and 6:00 p.m. I was beaten," Jordan stated. "I was permitted to rest over Sunday and

Monday, but on Tuesday, I was beaten again." Jordan named his assailants as detectives John Boston, Warren Murphy, Francis O'Connell, and police stenographer William Del Tore. Jordan claimed detectives took him to the scene of the crime and told him, step-by-step, just how the murder of Norman Bechtel took place. Only when detectives were satisfied that Jordan was well-rehearsed did they notify the mayor. If this was what really happened, it would explain the various inaccuracies in Jordan's confession and why Jordan was the one who had done most of the talking before the mayor.

While detectives adamantly denied these accusations on the witness stand, Dr. Harry Arkless, resident physician at the county prison, testified that Jordan was admitted to the facility with multiple bruises and several broken teeth. Since Jordan was held in isolation at the police station before his transfer to county prison, these injuries could have only been self-inflicted or inflicted at the hands of the mayor's notoriously corrupt detectives. The prosecution ended its case with a presentation of cigarette butts and matches found at the scene of the killing, which authorities cited as "proof" that Jordan had been on the grounds of the Stokes estate, as the butts were from a brand of cigarettes smoked by the defendant (apparently, Jordan must have been their only customer in the Philadelphia area).

At 9:28 in the evening, after three hours and thirty-three minutes of deliberation, a jury of six men and six women returned a verdict, convicting William Jordan of voluntary manslaughter, despite evidence that was flimsy at best. Ironically, the foreman of the jury was a realtor named Harry L. Bechtel, who claimed to be no relation to the victim. Jordan's attorney, Alexander Perry, asked for a deferred sentence, which was granted by Judge Millar. After the verdict had been returned, the other three defendants who were present during the trial—Fletcher Williams, Lucille Scott Young, and John Coles—were granted severance and released from custody. On August 26, Judge Millar refused Jordan's plea for a new trial and sentenced him to five to ten years at county prison.

DECISION REVERSED

Thanks to the efforts of William Jordan's attorney, the State Supreme Court reversed Judge Millar's decision and ordered a new trial, which took place on May 6, 1938. This time, the jury believed the chauffeur's claim that he had been beaten into giving a confession and that he had been coached on what to say in front of Mayor Wilson. After ninety minutes of deliberation, Jordan was acquitted and released from prison, thereby moving the Bechtel case back into the "unsolved" category, where it remains to this day.

In all probability, Jordan and Coles had something to do with the murder of Norman Bechtel, but, in this particular case, it was the very lawlessness of law enforcement which compromised the investigation. As to the identity of the person who plunged the long, deadly blade into the Mennonite church leader's chest, and whether or not this was the same person who carved occult symbols into the victim's face, this, unfortunately, will never be known. Too much time has passed, too much evidence has been lost or destroyed, and too many dirty hands have tainted the case.

In September of 1937, District Attorney Charles F. Kelly, partially inspired by the mishandling of the Bechtel case, requested a special grand jury to investigate corruption within the Philadelphia Police Department. Known as the "October Grand Jury" for when it was established, its series of hearings continued into March of 1939 and resulted in the immediate dismissal of Director of Public Safety Andrew J. Emanuel, who had held the position since the previous shake-up. Superintendent of Police Edward Hubbs was also relieved of duty, as were several other high-ranking members of the department. Ironically, the mayor who vowed to stamp out corruption was named in the grand jury's final report as one of the primary culprits responsible for police corruption, intimidation, and graft. When the press reached out to Mayor Wilson for comment, his reply was, simply, "No comment." He never faced repercussions for his oversight of the notoriously lawless Philadelphia Police Department; he died of a stroke three months after the October Grand Jury released its final report while still in office.

The victim's brother, Wilbur Rohrbach Bechtel, eventually returned to his home in Palm, Montgomery County, where he died in 1958, after a lengthy illness, at the age of fifty-four. After his death, it was reported that his estate was valued at just $885. Whatever became of the large windfall he had obtained as the beneficiary of Norman's will and life insurance policies? Did he gamble it away on bad investments like his brother? Was he pressured into loaning his fortune to corrupt law enforcement officials like Frank Choplinski who had no intention of ever paying it back? Or did he put the money to good use, caring for his crippled step-sister Elsie? This, too, is one of the myriad mysteries surrounding Philadelphia's most confounding murder.

Bibliography

1. THE FEELY TRIPLE DEATH MYSTERY

"Woman, Two Children Slain." *The Pittsburgh Press*. June 19, 1936.
"Hammer Print Clue in Family Slaying." *Pittsburgh Sun-Telegraph*. June 19, 1936.
"Triple Slaying Mystery Grows." *The Pittsburgh Press*. June 20, 1936.
"Triple Murder Theory Gaining." *Pittsburgh Post-Gazette*. June 20, 1936.
"Triple Death Probers Lean to Murder-Suicide." *The Pittsburgh Press*. June 21, 1936.
"Fingerprint May Be Key to Feely Crime." *Pittsburgh Post-Gazette*. June 24, 1936.
"Coroner Fails to Find Clues." *The Pittsburgh Press*. June 26, 1936.
"Quiz Nurse in Feely Slaying." *Pittsburgh Sun-Telegraph*. June 28, 1936.
"Suicide Theory Hit by Feely." *Pittsburgh Post-Gazette*. June 29, 1936.
"Police Continue Probe of Deaths." *The Pittsburgh Press*. July 2, 1936.
"Sleuths Close Feely Death Case." *Pittsburgh Sun-Telegraph*. July 2, 1936.
"Feely to Continue Probe in Triple Killing Theory." *The Pittsburgh Press*. July 10, 1936.
"Four Feely Motives Aired." *Pittsburgh Sun-Telegraph*. Aug 16, 1936.
"Feely Deaths Murder, Inspector Declares; Evidence Disappears." *The Pittsburgh Press*. Sep 13, 1936.
"Coroner Sets Date for Feely Inquest." *The Pittsburgh Press*. Nov 13, 1936.
"Witnesses Questioned by Feely." *Pittsburgh Sun-Telegraph*. Nov 24, 1936.
"Mrs. Feely Had Premonition of Death, Jury Told." *Pittsburgh Sun-Telegraph*. Nov 27, 1936.
"Mrs. Feely Murdered, Coroner's Jury Finds." *Pittsburgh Post-Gazette*. Nov 28, 1936.
"Feely Quits Post on Pitt Faculty." *The Pittsburgh Press*. Sep 12, 1937.
The Reporter Dispatch [White Plains, NY]. Death notices. May 22, 1995.

2. THE SKELETONS OF OYSTER PADDY'S TAVERN

"Fatal Saloon Row." *Pittsburgh Post-Gazette*. Aug 22, 1887.
"The Wound of Clerk 'Tiny' Sloan Proves Fatal." *Pittsburgh Post-Gazette*. Aug 23, 1887.
"Ask for First Degree; Commonwealth's Claim in the Sloan Murder Case." *The Pittsburgh Press*. May 15, 1888.
"Sloan's Last Statement." *The Pittsburgh Press*. May 16, 1888.
"An Old Dive Yields a Big Murder Mystery." *The Pittsburgh Press*. June 23, 1906.

"Old Dive Gives Up Its Dead." *The Pittsburgh Post*. June 23, 1906.
"Watch Adds to Evidence of Murders." *The Pittsburgh Press*. June 24, 1906.
"No Solution of Mystery." *The Pittsburgh Post*. June 24, 1906.
"Detectives Are Investigating Discovery of Two Skeletons." *Pittsburgh Post-Gazette*. June 24, 1906.
"Oyster Paddy Reported Dying." *The Pittsburgh Post*. March 20, 1907.
"Oyster Paddy Dies on Passenger Train." *The Pittsburgh Post*. April 15, 1907.

3. THE HOMETOWN FLAG DAY MASSACRE

"Wholesale Gang Killing Takes Three Lives at Hometown." *The Plain Speaker* [Hazleton, PA]. June 14, 1938.
"Police Identify Third Gang Killing Victim." *Hazleton Standard-Sentinel*. June 15, 1938.
"Three Men Murdered in Gang Massacre in Gaudy Room of Abandoned Roadhouse at Hometown, Mile North of Tamaqua." *Allentown Morning Call*. June 15, 1938.
"Hold Two for Questioning in Triple Murder." *Pottsville Republican*. June 15, 1938.
"Three Theories Advanced for Gang Slayings at Hometown; Inn Racket Headquarters." *The Plain Speaker* [Hazleton, PA]. June 15, 1938.
"Machine-Gunned in Roadhouse at Hometown, 3 Die." *The Times-Leader* [Wilkes-Barre, PA]. June 15, 1938.
"Police Fail to Find the Perpetrators of Hometown Flag Day Massacre." *The Record American* [Mahanoy City, PA]. June 15, 1938.
"Developments in Investigation in the Hometown Murders." *The Record American* [Mahanoy City, PA]. June 16, 1938.
"Shenandoah Man Questioned in Gang Massacre." *Hazleton Standard-Sentinel*. June 17, 1938.
"Jackman Still Held by Police." *The Plain Speaker* [Hazleton, PA]. June 17, 1938.
"Following the Trail of the Flag Day Slaughter at Hometown." *Mauch Chunk Times-News*. June 18, 1938.
"Police Question Murder Suspects." *The Record American* [Mahanoy City, PA]. June 18, 1938.
"Held Under $7,500 Bail in Hometown Slayings." *The Plain Speaker* [Hazleton, PA]. June 27, 1938.
"Body Found in Bootleg Hole Identified." *Allentown Morning Call*. July 15, 1938.
"Have New Angle Flag Day Case." *Pottsville Republican*. July 16, 1938.
"Shenandoah Man Is Charged With Triple Slaying." *Allentown Morning Call*. Nov 29, 1938.
"Shenandoah Man Held in Killings Remains in Jail." *Allentown Morning Call*. Nov 30, 1938.
"Hold Suspect in 1938 Massacre at Tamaqua Inn." *The Scranton Times*. Jan 17, 1940.
"Man Charged with Hometown Murders." *Shenandoah Evening Herald*. Jan 17, 1940.
"Suspect in Hometown Murder Case Released." *The Record American* [Mahanoy City, PA]. Jan 30, 1940.
"Roof of Home Adjoining Amber Lantern Hotel Is Badly Damaged by Fire." *Allentown Morning Call*. Aug 17, 1940.

"Unsolved Murders Pile Up during Whitehouse's Term." *The Record American* [Mahanoy City, PA]. Oct 28, 1941.

Evans, Elizabeth. "Gangsters, Guns & The Amber Lantern." *Pottsville Republican*. Jan 7, 1995.

4. THE HERSHEY TORCH MURDER

"Man Burns to Death in Auto Near Hershey." *The Patriot-News* [Harrisburg, PA]. Sep 24, 1928.

"Identity Still Puzzles; Various Clues Traced." *Harrisburg Telegraph*. Sep 25, 1928.

"Man Found Dead in Car Formerly of Pottsville." *Mount Carmel Item*. Sep 25, 1928.

"Man Burned in Auto Thought to Be Slain Reading Bootlegger." *Reading Times*. Sep 26, 1928.

"Cousin Finds Body Too Badly Charred to Tell Whether It Was Kaldes." *The Evening News* [Harrisburg, PA]. Sep 27, 1928.

"Slain Man's Cousin Quizzed 3 Hours." *Reading Times*. Sep 28, 1928.

"Fight to Get $25,000 Seen in Mystery Death." *Lancaster New Era*. Sep 27, 1928.

"Label Grave of Man Slain and Burned in Auto Unidentified." *Reading Times*. Sep 29, 1928.

"10 Men Try to Solve Flaming Auto Crime." *Reading Times*. Oct 1, 1928.

"Insurance Co. Requested an Examination." *Lebanon Daily News*. Oct 4, 1928.

"Haldos Charged with Murder and Fraud." *The Evening News* [Harrisburg, PA]. April 8, 1929.

"Torch Murder 'Victim' Sought." *Lancaster New Era*. April 8, 1929.

"Alleged Dead Man Skips Out." *Pottsville Republican*. April 8, 1929.

"Charles Kaldes Sought in Torch Murder Probe." *The Patriot-News* [Harrisburg, PA]. May 22, 1929.

"New Clues Found in Torch Killing." *Lancaster New Era*. May 22, 1929.

"Believe Solution Near in Hershey Murder Mystery." *Harrisburg Telegraph*. June 13, 1930.

"Grave Robbed for Torch Case Body." *The Evening News* [Harrisburg, PA]. June 20, 1930.

"Kaldes Confessed to Fraud Charge." *Lebanon Daily News*. June 21, 1930.

"Insurance Fraud Defendant Pleads." *The Scranton Republican*. July 8, 1930.

"2-Year Sentence Given Kaldes." *The Evening News* [Harrisburg, PA]. Sep 29, 1930.

5. THE WHITTMORE CASE

"Slayer Kills Pretty Girl." *Harrisburg Telegraph*. Sep 30, 1931.

"Mystery in City Woman's Death." *The Evening News* [Harrisburg, PA]. Sep 30, 1931.

"Mystery Veils Girl's Murder." *Harrisburg Telegraph*. Oct 1, 1931.

"Make Futile Search for Clue to Slayer of Pretty Divorcee." *Harrisburg Telegraph*. Oct 2, 1931.

"Bedroom Murder Is Unsolved." *Harrisburg Telegraph*. Oct 3, 1931.

"Five Charges Are Brought against Murder Witness." *Harrisburg Telegraph*. Oct 6, 1931.

"Police May Take Witness to Cleveland." *Harrisburg Telegraph*. Oct 7, 1931.

"Few Clues Found in Girl's Murder." *Harrisburg Telegraph*. Oct 14, 1931.

"Two Questioned in Doris Whittmore Slaying Again in Custody." *Harrisburg Telegraph*. Oct 30, 1931.

"Pinto Held on Three Charges." *Harrisburg Sunday Courier*. Feb 7, 1932.

"Ciallela to Face Charges in Court." *The Patriot-News* [Harrisburg, PA]. Feb 8, 1932.

"Year Old Mystery Murder of Girl Baffles Police." *Harrisburg Telegraph*. Sep 30, 1932.

"Pierce Girl Murder Mystery." *Harrisburg Telegraph*. April 10, 1933.

"Plea to Release Two from Murder Charge Refused." *Harrisburg Telegraph*. April 14, 1933.

"Two More to Be Released If $5000 Bail Is Furnished." *Harrisburg Telegraph*. April 17, 1933.

"Murder Trial Witness Tried for Burglary." *The Evening News* [Harrisburg, PA]. May 31, 1933.

"Ask Indictments in Slaying Today." *The Patriot-News* [Harrisburg, PA]. June 1, 1933.

"Grand Jury to Get Murder Charges." *The Patriot-News* [Harrisburg, PA]. Sep 8, 1933.

"Six to Be Cleared in Cherry Street Woman's Death." *Harrisburg Telegraph*. Sep 20, 1933.

"Accuse Second Man in Murder of Lucius Baker." *The Evening News* [Harrisburg, PA]. April 8, 1944.

"Sentences Four White Slavers." *The Evening Independent* [Massillon, OH]. Sep 18, 1942.

6. The Sugar Barrel Mystery

"One Clue in Murder Mystery; Medal of the Virgin Found Near the Body." *Wilkes-Barre Times*. Dec 17, 1906.

"Police Searched in Vain to Find a Definite Clew Barrel Murder Mystery." *The Wilkes-Barre News*. Dec 18, 1906.

"The Murder Mystery." *Hazleton Sentinel*. Dec 18, 1906.

"The Barrel Murder Mystery." *The Miner's Journal* [Pottsville, PA]. Dec 19, 1906.

"Slav Miner Charged with Being Implicated in Barrel Murder." *Mount Carmel Item*. Dec 19, 1906.

"Barrel Murder Mystery Reaches an Exceedingly Exciting Phase." *Wilkes-Barre Leader*. Dec 19, 1906.

"Mystery the Same; Anslovak Still Held." *Hazleton Sentinel*. Dec 19, 1906.

"Barrel Murder Mystery Deepens." *The Scranton Tribune*. Dec 19, 1906.

"Anslovak Released." *Hazleton Sentinel*. Dec 20, 1906.

"The Barrel Mystery Again." *Hazleton Sentinel*. Dec 29, 1906.

"Two Young Men Find Jewelry Worn by Victim." *The Daily Standard* [Hazleton, PA]. Jan 7, 1907.

"Clue to Barrel Murder." *The Philadelphia Inquirer*. Jan 20, 1907.

"May Clear Up Barrel Murder." *The Plain Speaker* [Hazleton, PA]. Aug 24, 1907.

"Butkiewicz and Jones Asked to Resign at the Request of Salsburg." *Wilkes-Barre Times Leader*. June 7, 1909.

"Barrel Mystery; Cruel Murder of Girl Being Revived." *The Daily Standard* [Hazleton, PA]. Jan 24, 1908.

"Man Thinks Body Found Was That of His Daughter." *The Philadelphia Inquirer*. Jan 26, 1908.

"Tried to Solve Barrel Mystery." *The Daily Standard* [Hazleton, PA]. Feb 11, 1908.

"Son of Famous Medium Ends Life." *The San Francisco Examiner*. Dec 21, 1908.

"Barrel Mystery May Soon Be Solved." *The Wilkes-Barre Record*. Feb 2, 1911.

"Local Detectives Believe They Have Clew to Identity of Victim." *Wilkes-Barre Semi-Weekly Record*. Aug 29, 1911.

7. THE BREAD MAN'S LAST DELIVERY

"Michael Wanzie Brutally Murdered." *Mount Carmel Item*. June 21, 1905.

"Robbers Foiled in an Attempt to Rob Restaurant." *The Shamokin Dispatch*. July 6, 1928.

"Truck Driver Is Mysteriously Missing; Drain Colliery Dam in Belief Local Man Met with Foul Play." *The Shamokin Dispatch*. May 2, 1932.

"Police Hold to Theory Claude Haas Is Alive." *The Shamokin Dispatch*. May 3, 1932.

"Auto Sought as Clue in the Haas Mystery." *The Shamokin Dispatch*. May 4, 1932.

"Cattle Rustlers Still Active in Trevorton Area." *The Shamokin Dispatch*. May 14, 1932.

"Donald Bastress Is Sought for Series of Daring Crimes." *The Shamokin Dispatch*. May 18, 1932.

"Bastress Confesses Wholesale Robberies." *The Shamokin Dispatch*. May 20, 1932.

"Daring Bandit Unfolds Crimes Under Grilling." *The Shamokin Dispatch*. May 21, 1932.

"Investigators Fail to Locate Body." *Weekly News-Sun* [Newport, PA]. Sep 22, 1932.

"Brutal Slaying of Claude Haas Revealed in Finding of Body in Old Mine Stable." *The Shamokin Dispatch*. July 18, 1933.

"Missing Truck Driver Slain; Badly Decomposed Body of Missing Claude Haas Found at Site of Former Stable." *Shamokin Daily News*. July 18, 1933.

"Think Bandit Holds Key to Tragic Death of Local Man." *The Shamokin Dispatch*. July 20, 1933.

"Bastress' Associate Gives Clue in Trevorton Mystery." *Shamokin Daily News*. July 31, 1933.

"Claude Haas Case Closed on Records as Unsolved." *The Shamokin Dispatch*. April 7, 1934.

"Bastress and Kessler Held in Theft Probe." *The Shamokin Dispatch*. April 14, 1941.

"Police Seek to Link Sunbury Holdup to Gang." *The Shamokin Dispatch*. April 21, 1941.

"Pair Pleads Guilty to Stealing Charges; Auctions Involved." *Pottstown Mercury*. Oct 7, 1952.

Obituary for Donald Bastress. *The Philadelphia Inquirer*. May 23, 1977.

8. THE LYCOMING CREEK TRAGEDY

"Mystery in Deaths of Shearer Couple Becoming Deeper." *The Philadelphia Inquirer*. July 21, 1922.

"Couple with Cut Throats in River; Williamsport Police Are Baffled by Strange Tragedy Revealed by Baby." *The Evening Times* [Sayre, PA]. July 20, 1922.

"Man and Wife Found in Creek, Throats Cut." *Lancaster New Era*. July 20, 1922.

"Murder, Suicide, Verdict." *The Buffalo Times*. July 21, 1922.

"No Clue to Mystery of Couple's Death." *The News-Journal* [Lancaster, PA]. July 21, 1922.

"Identify Bodies of Slayer and His Wife." *The Plain Speaker* [Hazleton, PA]. July 21, 1922.

"No Clue to Tragedy of Lycoming Creek." *York Daily Record*. July 21, 1922.

"Mystery Around Double Tragedy Baffles Police." *Harrisburg Telegraph*. July 21, 1922.

"Shearer Insane, Says Wife's Kin." *Evening Public Ledger* [Philadelphia, PA]. July 21, 1922.

"Tot's Talk Solves Murder Mystery." *The Philadelphia Inquirer*. July 22, 1922.

"Henry Shearer Buried Today." *Harrisburg Telegraph*. July 24, 1922.

"Two New Clues Fail to Clear Death of Pair." *Harrisburg Telegraph*. July 25, 1922.

"Nearly 1000 People at the Funeral of Late Henry Shearer." *Lebanon Daily News*. July 25, 1922.

"Mystery Surrounds Pairs' Tragic Death." *The Lancaster News-Journal*. July 26, 1922.

"State Police Now Trying to Solve Mystery; Knife Found on Dead Man's Body Not One He Purchased from Troy Dealer." *Harrisburg Telegraph*. July 26, 1922.

"Believe Shearer Killed Wife in Fit of Insanity." *Harrisburg Telegraph*. July 27, 1922.

"State Police Now Check Over Evidence to Prove Shearer Committed Crime." *Harrisburg Telegraph*. July 28, 1922.

"Probe Shows That Shearer Slew His Wife." *The Evening News* [Wilkes-Barre, PA]. July 28, 1922.

"Jealousy Caused Deaths of Two; State Police Hold Opinion That Shearer Killed Wife and Then Self." *The Morning Press* [Bloomsburg, PA]. July 29, 1922.

"Orphaned Child Sheds New Light on the Grim Tragedy." *The Semi-Weekly News* [Lebanon, PA]. July 31, 1922.

9. THE MURDER OF MARGARET MARTIN

"Missing Kingston Girl Slain." *The Philadelphia Inquirer*. Dec 22, 1938.

"Trapper Finds Martin Girl's Body in Stream." *The Scranton Times*. Dec 22, 1938.

"Body of Missing Girl Is Found Under Bridge 30 Miles from Kingston." *Allentown Morning Call*. Dec 22, 1938.

"Mutilated Body of Kingston Girl Is Found in Burlap Sack, Stripped, Strangled by White Slave Agents." *The Morning Press* [Bloomsburg, PA]. Dec 22, 1938.

"Kidnap Victim Killed; Body Found." *Gazette and Bulletin* [Williamsport, PA]. Dec 22, 1938.

"Missing Girl Slain; Find Her Body in a Creek." *The Patriot* [Harrisburg, PA]. Dec 22, 1938.

"Mad Killer's Description Spurs Police Hunt for Girl's Slayer." *Pottstown Mercury*. Dec 23, 1938.

"Missing Girl Murdered and Body Hid in Culvert." *The Mountain Echo* [Shickshinny, PA]. Dec 23, 1938.

"Girl's Killer and His Car Described; Identification Expected within a Day." *The Scranton Tribune*. Dec 23, 1938.

"Autopsy Shows Degenerate Is Slayer of Girl." *The Morning Press* [Bloomsburg, PA]. Dec 23, 1938.

"Trace Burlap Sack to Mill." *The Morning Press* [Bloomsburg, PA]. Dec 27, 1938.

"Kingston Man Now Linked to Martin Murder." *The Scranton Tribune*. Dec 28, 1938.

"State Police Push Search for Murderer." *Evening Herald* [Shenandoah, PA]. Dec 29, 1938.

"Comb Woodland for Clues in Martin Slaying." *The Scranton Tribune*. Dec 29, 1938.

"Murderer Not Found; State Police Question Many in Search for Slayer of Margaret Martin." *Tunkhannock New Age*. Dec 29, 1938.

"Mill Believed Martin Death Scene." *The Scranton Tribune*. Dec 30, 1938.

"Sawmill Clue Is Abandoned in Kingston Murder Case." *The Scranton Tribune*. Jan 3, 1939.

"Says He Killed Kingston Girl, Not Miss Martin." *Reading Times*. Jan 17, 1939.

"Foremost Suspect in Martin Killing Gives Iron-Clad Alibi." *The Scranton Tribune*. Feb 8, 1939.

"No Martin Murder Clues After 2 Month Man-Hunt." *The Plain Speaker* [Hazleton, PA]. Feb 15, 1939.

"Morals Cases Rise." *Evening Herald* [Shenandoah, PA]. March 2, 1939.

"Martin Murder Suspect Freed; Woman Claims Man Offered Job and Took Long Motor Trip with Her." *The Plain Speaker* [Hazleton, PA]. April 11, 1939.

"Schedule Conference on Reward for Slayer." *The Scranton Times*. June 23, 1939.

"Arrest 2 Men Near Scene of Murder of Margaret Martin." *The Plain Speaker* [Hazleton, PA]. Aug 5, 1939.

"C.W. Schooley Faces Charges." *Wilkes-Barre Record*. Aug 28, 1939.

"State Puts 'Ace' on Martin Case." *Pittsburgh Sun-Telegraph*. Oct 13, 1939.

"Admits Martin Murder, Then Changes Story." *The Scranton Tribune*. Sep 19, 1942.

"Police Await Replies on Queries Sent Out in Martin Murder Case." *The Scranton Times*. Sep 21, 1942.

"Inmate Dead, 2 Others Ill from Poison Cocktails." *Elmira Star-Gazette*. May 25, 1944.

10. THE EVIL EYE KILLER

Garber, John Palmer, et al. *History of Old Germantown: With a Description of Its Settlement and Some Account of Its Important Persons, Buildings and Places Connected with Its Development*. United States, H. F. McCann, 1907.

Mawhinney, George. "Man Beaten and Stabbed to Death in Germantown." Mawhinney, George. *The Philadelphia Inquirer*. Jan 20, 1932.

Mawhinney, George. "Brand of Death Slashed on Victim's Body Starts Search for Mad Slayer." *The Philadelphia Inquirer*. Jan 21, 1932.

"Think Bechtel Slayers Erred Choosing Victim." *Allentown Morning Call*. Jan 21, 1932.

Mawhinney, George. "Police to Seek Death Clue in Bechtel Will." *The Philadelphia Inquirer*. Jan 22, 1932.

"Cult Sacrifice Clues Sought in Bechtel Murder." *Reading Times*. Jan 22, 1932.

"Police without Clue to Slayer of Churchman." *Allentown Morning Call*. Jan 22, 1932.

Mawhinney, George. "Dodge Board Probes Killing of Churchman." *The Philadelphia Inquirer*. Jan 23, 1932.

Mawhinney, George. "Bechtel Eye Gouged Out by Slayer." *The Philadelphia Inquirer*. Jan 24, 1932.

"Bechtel Murder in Philadelphia Recalls Slaying of Mabel Bechtel." *Allentown Morning Call*. Jan 24, 1932.

"Bechtel Youth Is Scanned for Clue to Death." *The Philadelphia Inquirer*. Jan 25, 1932.

"Eye-Mark Murder Key Now Sought from Woman." *The Philadelphia Inquirer*. Jan 26, 1932.

Mawhinney, George. "Bechtel Death Probe Turns to Second Woman." *The Philadelphia Inquirer*. Jan 27, 1932.

"$1000 Reward Offered for Bechtel's Slayer." *The Philadelphia Inquirer*. Feb 3, 1932.

"Bechtel Will Benefits 2 Mennonite Churches." *The Philadelphia Inquirer*. Feb 4, 1932.

"New Bechtel Clue Leads to Jail Cell." *The Philadelphia Inquirer*. Feb 9, 1932.

"Bechtel Inquest Set for Next Wednesday." *The Philadelphia Inquirer*. Feb 10, 1932.

"Bechtel Reward Posters Torn Down." *The Philadelphia Inquirer*. Feb 11, 1932.

"Coroner's Inquiry Fails to Reveal Bechtel's Slayer." *The Philadelphia Inquirer*. Feb 18, 1932.

"Cult Is New Clue in Bechtel Slaying." *The Philadelphia Inquirer*. Feb 21, 1932.

"Cult Threat Bared by Forte's Widow; Members Named." *The Philadelphia Inquirer*. Feb 23, 1932.

"Recalls Bechtel Death." *The Philadelphia Inquirer*. Aug 16, 1932.

"Crime Prober Slain in Row; Hunt Suspect." *The Philadelphia Inquirer*. Dec 8, 1932.

"Hunt Spreads for Slayer of City Detective." *The Philadelphia Inquirer*. Dec 9, 1932.

"Police Face Shake-Up from Dodge Down." *The Philadelphia Inquirer*. Dec 11, 1932.

"Sugarfoot Confesses He Slew Croskey." *The Philadelphia Inquirer*. Dec 11, 1932.

"Court Adjudicates Estate of Bechtel, Mysteriously Slain." *The Philadelphia Inquirer*. May 31, 1933.

"Weird Bechtel Cult Murder Unsolved after 5 Year Hunt." *The Philadelphia Inquirer*. Jan 19, 1937.

Mawhinney, George. "Eye Murder of 1932 Solved by Confession of Chauffeur." *The Philadelphia Inquirer*. April 15, 1937.

Bartlett, Dorothy. "Mayor Grills Bechtel's Kin; Charges Move to Drop Case." *The Philadelphia Inquirer*. April 16, 1937.

"Murder of Bechtel Is Solved without Single New Clue." *The Philadelphia Inquirer*. April 18, 1937.

"Bechtel Prisoners Moved." *The Philadelphia Inquirer*. April 21, 1937.

"Razor Blade Found in Suspect's Coat." *The Philadelphia Inquirer*. April 23, 1937.

"Seek New Witness in Bechtel Murder." *The Philadelphia Inquirer*. April 24, 1937.

"New Evidence Puts Woman at Scene of Bechtel Murder." *The Philadelphia Inquirer*. April 29, 1937.

"Jury Convicts Chauffeur in Bechtel Case." *The Philadelphia Inquirer*. May 21, 1937.

"Jailed 10 Years in Bechtel Slaying." *The Philadelphia Inquirer*. Aug 27, 1937.

"High Court Hears Bechtel Appeal." *The Philadelphia Inquirer*. Dec 3, 1937.

McDonnell, Owen. "Crime Jury Hits Police and Wilson as Corrupt." *The Philadelphia Inquirer*. March 2, 1939.

"County Coroner Terms Death in Palm a Suicide." *Pottstown Mercury*. Nov 8, 1958.

About the Author

Marlin Bressi is the host and creator of the *Pennsylvania Oddities* true crime and paranormal podcast and the author of *Hairy Men in Caves: True Stories of America's Most Colorful Hermits* (Sunbury Press, 2015). His fiction has appeared in *Suspense Magazine, Black Cat Mystery Magazine, Sherlock Holmes Mystery Magazine, Mystery Tribune,* and other publications. He currently resides in Harrisburg, Pennsylvania.